The Agape Spectrum

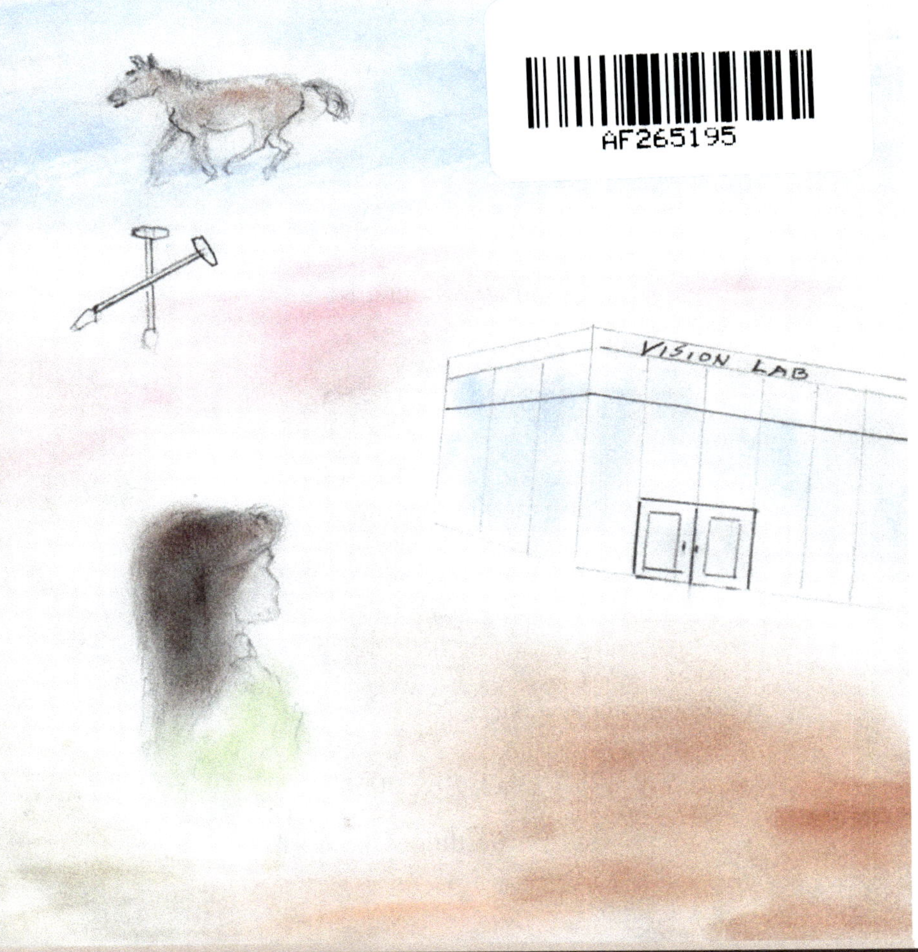

By James Michael Ruether

ISBN 0-932218-73-3

Published at Devore, CA by

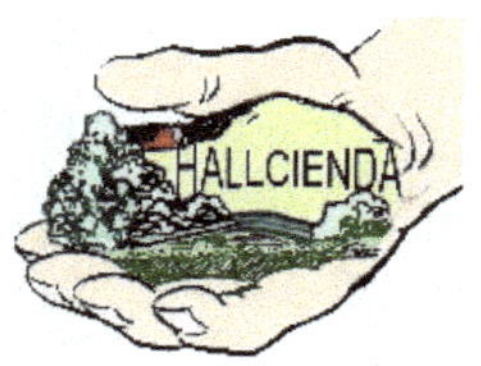

P.O. Box 9066

San Bernardino, CA 92427

ACKNOWLEDGMENTS

Jerri

Jerri and her family are loved by my family, and we made trouble here in Chino, California 30+ years ago—fun and unforgettable memories were made together. Our houses were full of joy and laughter whenever we got together. The volume of life was turned up. Mike played his guitar, and Jerri and all would sing with wonderful voices.

The memories were priceless gifts to my family that money can't buy. Now it's my turn to open my imagination and create my gift to Jerri and her family that is of really no monitory value— just Agape saying thank you from my heart.

Agape Spectrum is the result—Jerri's haunting fiction story of demons, ghosts, and splattered brains on bedroom walls. From her dreams to reality she will live them all.

Brianne Hawks

Brianne is the expert on horses from whom I acquired my information for this story. Bentley and Mini Cooper are her horses. She is my friend and the best real estate agent around. I gave her a colorful role in this story for helping me, and now she is in a published book. Thank you, Brianne.

Bill Boyd

Bill Boyd has competed in the Transpacific Yacht Race and is an expert captain in high demand. He was my informational resource on the yacht types, speed, and navigation. Bill is also the best real estate broker and client portfolio investor in the California coastal area and Hawaii.

Bill is Hawaiian and is a hero in my book and to many in life. Thank you so much Bill for your contribution to The Agape Spectrum.

Special Thanks to

Mentor, friend, editor, publisher, Alice Hall and to
My wife Deana, and Alice's son Stephen for meticulous proofing.

Agape

(Ancient Greek ἀγάπη, agapē) is a Greco-Christian term referring to love, "the highest form of love, charity" and "the love of God for man and of man for God".

Have you
  Ever wondered
   what the
    World looks like
     Through Gods Eyes ?

Table of Contents

The Characters

The starring roll of the vision scientist is played by Jerri

Her loving sister is Jan

Detective: Richard Michaels / deceased wife, Crystal

Clients: Agnes; Jesús and his Mom and Dad

Mule Kick Saloon and stable friend: Brianne Hawks

Officer: Steve Ross

Chef: Fabian Spadazzi

Cowboy: Luke Grieves

Restaurant owner: Giovanni

Receptionist: Cassi

Veterinarian: Dr. Jack Clark / wife, Carolann

Richard's maid: Grace

Sail boat Captain: Bill Boyd / daughter Anakalia

Rodeo Vet: Dr. Stanton aka Rocky the rodeo clown

Mule Kick Saloon bartender: Buck

Horses: Starring Bentley, Mini Cooper; Tux in a supporting roll

Stable dog: Sally

Stable Cats: Just Cats

Jan has stable friends and the ones not at the stable we will call her unstable friends; can't share their identity unless I accidently slip up or maybe I could just point at one.

Chapter 1
Murder in Ocean Crest

Ocean Crest is a boring town of simplicity with no sense of worry or dread, but tonight that is all to be over. Your blood will be spilled in your bed. No one in this town is safe, so on your pillow lay your sweet head. Before morning sun rises you surely will be dead! I have excited the evil demons that whirl around in my head. I seek tonight to have her to myself as she's sleeping in her bed. Crystal should never have rejected me with the words that she said, so tonight I will have my way with this bitch before I smash the brains out of her head!

Life is a bit slower in the town of Ocean Crest. There are the very rich, and at the other end of the spectrum, the not so rich. The people of Ocean Crest enjoy the cool ocean breezes, and it is common to see the town folks walk and browse through the little shops lining the old town streets. Others relax with the sound of wine glasses clinking in the various open air jazz clubs in the evening with friends sharing a glass of wine and interesting conversation—like the story of a town shaking an unsolved horrific murder five years in the past.

Ocean Crest boasts a mixture of residential, beach, agricultural, and equestrian estates, all in this tightknit community, where everyone shares a rapport with each other as they all rely on the talents of neighbors. There's a country dance saloon located near the equestrian/agricultural part of town that caters to the wilder bunch. If you have a smart mouth, there you will receive a well-deserved ass kickin', I promise.

This quiet little town is going to get shook up again, and Jerri's life is about to get real!

Jerri has had a hard week at The Vision Lab she owns. Today was especially hard, and not because of a man who calls himself the Fly Guy, who buzzed in to pick up his quadrifocals. Yes, there are a few of these types in Ocean Crest, and they dress the part. The Fly Guy? Well, he thinks he can see like a fly, so Dr. Jerri will humor him. It really can't hurt, and she makes a buck. Everyone is happy. She hands him his glasses, and he smiles as he buzzes off.

But there is a little five-year-old boy named Jesús that visited the office today to pick up a new pair of glasses.

"Jerri! Doctor Jerri!" The sweet young voice of li'l Jesús shatters the calm. He bursts in with a smile and a laugh, wearing his cowboy boots and his John Deere Farm hat that he is so proud of. It's just like the one his daddy wears.

His mother Juanita brings him into the office every three months, as the vision of this little five-year-old is gradually failing from a disease with no cure. He will be completely blind in a few more years. Although poor, Juanita always brings Jerri a variety of a dozen freshly made, very delicious tamales to each office visit. Jerri does not charge this family for services. She loved them from their first visit. Juanita offered her free house cleaning for trade, but Jerri declined and said she should spend her time with her son Jesús—he needs her.

Jerri holds Jesús on her lap at each visit. He hops up on her lap because they were friends from the start. They speak *un poquito* bit of Spanish to each other, as of course, Jesús loves to teach his friend, Jerri, his language. And she brings him his favorite Mexican candy, marzipan covered with chocolate.

Jesús is her favorite client because, even at only 45, she has grandchildren his age, and that makes it harder for her to see his sight decline. His father works hard as a foreman in the farm industry to make ends meet, but there is little chance for advancement beyond that in this industry. It is mostly seasonal work.

"Jerri!" Jesús shouts with excitement, "My Papa got two trucks to take vegetables from the farm to the place to sell 'um. I love to ride with him to do that. He says I will drive one when I get big like him. He got my name on the trucks' doors—says Jesús and Son Trucking. I am Li'l Jesús—that means son." Jesús roars, making truck sounds, turning his arms like he is driving.

"That is wonderful, Jesús. You guys are living the American dream, building for a bright future".

Juanita just smiles and holds her hands as if in prayer and looks up and shrugs her shoulders.

Well, it's the end of the work day, and Jesús is her last patient, so she bids Jesús an adios, and he tips his li'l hat and waves back at her with his chocolate smeared hand and smiling face.

* * * * *

Jerri walks into her office as a nightmare flashback suddenly shoots fear through her. She falls into her desk chair. She holds onto the desk tightly, shaking until her paralyzing vision goes away.

Why am I having this damn dream when I am awake? It's bad enough when I'm asleep. I have to find a way to stop it. I need an answer, Jerri thinks to herself. *What is this beach sand doing on the office floor, looks like someone's finger wrote Agape in it. What the hell is that? This has to be swept up.* She frowns.

This modern vision care facility is located in a storefront building next to an Italian restaurant and a real estate office. This vision care facility is different from all the others in that they create the glasses from raw materials—they forge silica sand into glass and grind their own glass lenses in-house.

Grabbing her purse and keys, Jerri locks up and walks away from her nightmarish vision to her car, another week behind her. She walks to her personal parking space that has painted checkered flags on a sign at the curb, since she's a lover of speed. She approaches her new red 2019 Jaguar XE SV. No one can catch her—she has 592 hp under that hood.

Jerri is impeccably dressed under her lab coat. Her long brown hair hangs loose and displays a few silver streaks of wisdom. And this only enhances her beauty.

The "pedal to the metal" drive home is short in this car,

and she feels the need to relax. She plans to spend a quiet day at her favorite secret spot on the beach tomorrow near where a stream enters into the ocean, so she can collect her thoughts; and maybe she will sing some oldies.

Jerri has a beautiful singing voice and could have been a famous singer; however sometimes dreams in life slip away like in the surf, trying to hold sand in your fist when the ocean waves hit you. The tighter you squeeze your fist, the faster the sand slips away through your fingers. The pounding waves of our lives leave us just standing alone, emptyhanded. Life's disappointments can get heavy with carrying all the "but onlys" and "what ifs" of life in the backs of our minds. We tell ourselves *don't look back at our past disappointments*, but then the waves of life smack us right in the face again. We tumble under life's surf once more. We climb back up empty-handed, finding the sinking sand moving away under our feet.

We put on our best Hollywood smile for a while, but our thinking goes right back again to the "but onlys" and "what ifs" of our lives. *I guess we will ponder our "but-only-what-ifs" all of our todays and on through our tomorrows*, Jerri thinks as she wheels her Jag through the gates.

Upon arriving at her estate, her younger sister Jan meets her at their entry by the big, tall, wooden front doors, smiling, ready to share her exciting day at the Polo club with Jerri. Jan loves her sister so much, she hugs and leans on her, kind of like a lovable yellow Labrador retriever, all slobbery like, and Jerri loves Jan, too.

"Hi, Jan, I got your text. You can share your day with me after my bath. I can't wait to hear what happened!"

"Cool, Sis. Yes, we had some disabled children visit us at the stables today, it was heartwarming—the gentle reaction the horses showed to the children. I will give you details later and have your tea ready for you with our dinner."

Jerri walks down the cool polished marble floor hallway

toward her master suite to draw a bath. This elegant estate has bright walls, tall ceilings with oil paintings and elegant tapestries on the bright walls, illuminated by the light beaming through the tall arched windows.

This early 1900s modernized Spanish estate has dark secrets of its own, complete with rumors of bumps and shadows in the night that every overnight guest will soon experience. Jerri purchased this estate at an astonishingly low price, for some reason, five years ago. The estate spans five thousand square feet of living area in a single story with open concept and is the envy of many of those who entertain. The master suite opens to a private secluded garden with a spa made of stone fitted into the surroundings.

After her bath and a small meal while catching up with Jan's rewarding day, Jerri retires to her room to enjoy a book in her bed before turning out the light.

Saturday morning comes soon, and she collects her beach stuff and tamales for lunch for a well-deserved relaxing day of perfect seclusion. Jerri brings her grandchildren's sand bucket and shovel—maybe to make a sand castle at her special secret spot on the beach. It is a beautiful morning full of promise, and the waves crash onto the shore with roars, sending up sprays of ocean fragrance that fill the air.

Jerri parks her car. The short dirt path that she walks ends at the sand. She steps out of her sandals hurriedly to squish her painted toes in the soft cool morning sand. Looking out over the powerful ocean, Jerri takes a deep breath with arms up over her head. Lowering them, her face beams into a big smile.

What a great day this has started out to be. The ice plant flowers bloom their bright shiny red colors. Unfolding her beach chair that has seen better days, but which holds a nostalgic dear memory in her heart that comforts her, Jerri spreads her beach supplies around the chair in very strategic positions just at arm's reach. She settles into her chair on the sand and opens a new book on travels that she would like to take some day. She has the time today to dream of faraway places and close her eyes to just imagine being there.

Pushing her heels deep into the sand to adjust the position of her chair to the perfect angle of comfort, she opens her book. The page lands on photos of Greece, and her imagination takes her there. The sun breaks through morning clouds, caressing her face with its warmth, enticing a small smile to emerge under her Prada sunglasses.

After an hour or so of relaxing, she feels a tap on her shoulder. She looks around, but nobody is there. *Wow, that's weird! I wonder who touched me. Oh well, I think I will take a walk up the stream bed to see the rabbits hopping and the birds that are singing to me this morning.* Venturing farther up the stream bed she sees a flash of light and then an aura of rainbow reflections of light that sparkle around on the stream bank. *Wow, what is that? I feel so good coming closer to it.*

Carrying the bucket and shovel in her hand, she walks up to the area and discovers a little pile of perfectly pure silica sand that throws little rainbow reflections dancing up on the banks of the stream bed. Jerri hasn't seen anything like this before. The sand, with colors moving around inside it, seems to have powers of its own.

I would like to make a pair of glasses out of this silica sand, as it has special properties, she thinks aloud to herself. *It's as if one of God's angels has touched the sand with its toe, energizing it with God's power at this very spot. I wonder what kind of lenses I could grind out of this sand.*

Jerri is a very intelligent, creative person with doctorates in both physical science and ophthalmology as her background, but she is private and keeps to herself outside the office, not trying to bring any attention her way. She keeps everybody in her life at arm's length with the exception of Jan and Li'l Jesús. Perhaps, someone betrayed her trust in the past, so her personal space includes the emotional one also. No one gets past her smile.

She collects a bucket full of the energized sand, which vibrates in the bucket as if it contains awesome power. *I will take this to my lab on Monday. I can't wait to share this with Sis because sparkly things like this will mesmerize Jan into a trance like a cat watching a fish bowl.*

The weekend is short, but seems long to Jerri, who is eager to get to the lab, hoping to unlock the special properties of the sand she has collected. *I'm going to store most of the sand at home and bring to work enough to make a pair of glasses.*

Monday morning, Jerri opens the office and enters. Carrying her purse, lunch bag, and container of sand, she hurriedly scrambles into the office, almost knocking over a tall green plant in the waiting room, catching it just in time, as she rushes past reception and into the lab.

Starting the forge, she turns on the office lights and puts the coffee on while waiting for the forge to heat up. She paces back and forth in anticipation. Okay, now its time!

She inserts the rainbow sand into the forge, and it turns into a liquid full of colors swirling around within it. Jerri pours the liquid into the lens forms to cool before grinding them into the shape that matches her eye sight. After they cool, Jerri grinds and polishes the lenses to fit common black frames.

Now Jerri inspects the glasses, and the lenses appear to have a prism of colors moving around inside the glass. *Wow! these glass lenses are energized with power—quite unusual.*

Jerri puts the glasses on and looks through them. Something happens in her heart. As she watches people on the sidewalk strolling by, she actually feels love and compassion for complete strangers. In fact, she is able to see the emotional pain or happiness in their hearts. This scares the hell out of her, so she removes the glasses immediately.

After placing them on her desk, she pulls an old book from the bookcase. This book she remembered from a college class, spoke of a spectrum of light that may open up a window to God's heart, but that was just a theory. There's a puzzled look on her face as she dusts off the book and opens it. The table of contents has a chapter called *The Agape Spectrum, a Window to God's Love.*

The book states a belief that if that particular spectrum of invisible light could be made visible somehow, the visibility would open the Agape Spectrum of light into what is God's love, because God is Love and also the Light of life.

Jerri reads this and looks at the glasses to watch the energized colors move around through the lenses. She wonders, *did I find the substance to make visible the invisible light spectrum that has power to see people's hearts with compassion and love beyond our human capacity?*

Jerri puts the glasses on again and walks up to the mirror, where she sees a child's reflection of herself as a little girl again. This reflection reveals the broken little girl that's hidden inside herself. She wants to forgive this sad, little girl-image weeping in the mirror, but instead she realizes the little girl inside her is innocent and isn't to blame for the things of her past.

She sees the love inside herself, buried behind all the pain of her past for so long. Small tears well up in Jerri's eyes and streak down her cheeks. She starts to love herself again. The pain in her past is healing in her heart by an overwhelming feeling of love. It is like she is being hugged by the loving arms of God. Her knees feel weak. As she looks at her mirror tear-streaked face reflection, something amazing happens. The lines on her face are disappearing.

Oh my, these glasses have a healing effect. I have never felt so much love in my life before now. She crosses her hands over her heart trying to contain her love.

Jerri is learning that these glasses she made are letting in a little bit of God's light in the world she views. She had read that God is Light and Love. Could this be happening? Like seeing the world through God's eyes, if only by just a little bit.

She looks sharply in the mirror and notices that she looks ten years younger. And she feels stronger. *I wonder if these glasses will heal my little friend, Jesús. I've got to get myself together now and fix my makeup.*

Jerri puts the glasses in her Lab coat and walks to the waiting room. Her next patient, Agnes, an elderly English lady, is walking into the office grumbling to her daughter. Agnes can no longer drive because of her failing eyesight so her daughter chauffeurs her around to her appointments dutifully.

"Good morning, Agnes," Jerri greets her.

"Good morning, Dear," Agnes grumbles as she shuffles in with her walker.

"Come on back to room #3, and I will bring your new prescription glasses in for you to try on."

Jerri wants to test the special glasses on Agnes first, so she says, "Agnes, I want you to try on these black-rimmed glasses to compare your sight with your new ones."

Agnes says, "Okay, Dear, if I must."

Jerri places the glasses on her face. "Oh, dear, Dr. Jerri," Agnes gushes, "what is this feeling of happiness? My vision is becoming clearer as the moments go by. What are these glasses?"

"Oh, they are something I am experimenting with on a select few patients that have more advanced sight loss."

"Doctor, I can now see perfectly and precisely, and I feel so much love for everyone today," Agnes whispers.

Her daughter says, "Mum, you are mostly a grumpy Gus! What happened?"

Jerri says, "I think a look through these glasses made her happy that she can see better."

Agnes laughs. "My back doesn't hurt anymore, and I am stronger."

"Okay," Jerri says, "let me put those glasses back in my pocket for now."

"What just happened Doctor? I can see perfectly without glasses at all," Agnes shouts.

Jerri shushes her. "We have to keep this a secret for now, so please, don't tell a soul and come back in two weeks. I want to see if your eyesight has stabilized. Okay?"

"Oh, yes, Doctor! I feel wonderful! I don't need this damn, blasted walker anymore more either." Agnes leaves the office almost skipping out as her daughter, looking puzzled, folds up the walker her mom left behind. "Oh, boy, Doctor! Whatever you did to her, I thank you, but I don't understand it."

Jerri said, "This is a new and harmless experimental treatment I am testing with my favorite patients. So, remember, not a word to anyone! Please."

"Don't worry. I won't tell anyone, Doctor."

"I believe she may not need glasses anymore, but I need to have a follow up visit to monitor her. Okay?"

"Yes, Doctor. In a fortnight we will return."

Jerri turns and goes into her private office to take it all in. *What have I discovered?* she asks herself. *This is frightening to possess something with powers beyond my comprehension. Did I just open Pandora's Box? But mythical Pandora's Box was filled with curses, and the glasses appear to be blessings. But what a great responsibility to possess. I must move forward very cautiously from now on and test them on myself in brief moments.*

The next client coming through the door looks like Clark Kent of the Superman series; quite striking in appearance in his white shirt and black tie with the shirt sleeves folded up to just below his elbows. Rumors around town are that he is troubled, and his temper has become explosive over these past few years.

"Good morning, Detective Michaels. How are you this morning?" Jerri asked.

"Oh, Doctor, you don't have to address me as Detective, you can call me Richard. And, by the way, I am splendid this morning and am looking forward getting my new glasses because it is that time of year again for qualifying with my service weapon."

"Well then, you don't have to call me Doctor. Just call me Jerri."

"Ah, I am impressed. I may need to bow to you because your name means 'Ruler with Spear'."

Jerri laughs. "Is that so, Richard? In that case, I think I will now take charge of this appointment," she smiles. "Okay, Richard, right this way into room #2 for you, and I will return with your glasses."

"Well, okay, Jerri, you're the boss."

Chapter 2
No Closure for Crystal

Detective Michaels has been on the force for over twenty years and has been honored because of a number of heroic actions. He is referred to as "Superman" by his fellow officers; however he is humble about it. Five years ago, while he was on a stakeout one night, his wife, Crystal, was raped and murdered in their home by someone in a ski mask with a scorpion tattoo on his right forearm that was caught on the surveillance camera. These images were shown on the news broadcast at the time for anyone who could identify the murderer, but he has never been caught. Richard feels he will never rest until he brings that man to justice. Needless to say, his demeanor has suffered since his loss.

"Here they are Richard. You try these glasses on, and we will see if your vision is improved," Jerri says briskly as she returns to the room.

Richard slips them on and nods. "Jerri, with these glasses I will qualify easily."

"Very good. I'm glad you trusted me to spearhead your care if you get my point," Jerri snickers.

"Oh, it is my high honor, Your Highness!" Richard guffaws. "Jerri, I haven't had a laugh for a while now, and it is a very refreshing break from all the seriousness of life. I look forward to my next visit, and here is my card just in case someone causes you any trouble. I am at your service, Your Highness." He bows slightly and grins.

"Thank you, Richard, I'm happy to clear up your eyesight and put a smile on your heart this morning."

And then, just as fast as he arrived as Clark Kent, he flies away like Superman to save the city—in Jerri's imagination.

This has been a very interesting morning, Jerri thinks to herself. *I remember the horror like yesterday—the tragic murder of Mrs. Michaels. I can see Richard has poured his life into his work to hide from his pain.* Jerri has been married a few times now with little success and is looking for the right man who can fill the emptiness in her heart. She ignores the butterfly feeling in her stomach and the hope in her heart that wants to see Richard again. *I hope he can find peace. I wonder if I could help him find it? Oh, there I go again—trying to fix another troubled man!* Jerri thinks with calm compassion as she slips on the Agape glasses and muses.

Now, my thoughts on these glasses—they have the power to allow me to see the joy, but also all the sorrow, and it is almost unbearable, watching the busy world of people scurrying around looking down at their phone texts. Most are feeling lonely, desperate, and empty inside. They are hoping that the person on the other end of the text really loves them and believes that they will fill the emptiness they have in their hearts. I can kinda see the faces of the people they are texting, and some are boy or girlfriends, moms, dads, children, or just a friend to lean on.

Through my glasses the sadness shows like a dark purple cloud around the heart area. Scared is like a brown cloud. Red is angry. Happy is a yellow cloud around the heart area. People with white clouds around the heart are hard because nothing is revealed. Is that because they are pure or victorious? But evil is like a black whirling cloud. It's scary that I can see their thoughts and what they have done like a movie in my mind. I want to take my eyes or mind off them, but it's like a train wreck. I can't look away. I have almost become addicted now. Is it better to live life in the dark, not knowing what these glasses reveal? But not wearing them feels like driving a car blindfolded.

Richard's heart area doesn't show the emotional feeling revealed like all the others. It is hidden from me for some reason. But I see in his eyes the pain he is holding. I think I will put these in my pocket for now and take a break.

Maybe I will go to Palermo's Italian Restaurant next door for lunch; they have wonderful Alfredo. I believe I have earned a glass of wine today also.

"Cassi, I will be next door for lunch," Jerri tells her receptionist as she approaches the door to the street.

"Thank you, Doctor. Enjoy your lunch."

Jerri removes her Lab coat, puts her glasses in her purse and walks to the restaurant.

"Hello Doctor," the robust Giovanni, the restauranteur, greets her, "I have your special booth for you right over here."

"Thank you, Gio, my dear. I will have my usual with a glass of your best, of course."

"Yes, it is on the way as we speak."

"You are the best, Gio!"

"I am honored with your presence, Doctor Jerri," Giovanni smiles.

The aroma of the complementary garlic bread sticks fills the air, and the bouquet of the rich red wine swirling in her glass brings a smile to her face as relaxation covers her like a warm blanket.

"Here is your entrée, Doctor, please enjoy."

"Thank you, Gio. By the way; in your busy kitchen is that a new chef with black hair and a tattoo on his right forearm that I see?"

"Yes, Fabian has moved back to this area. He just graduated from culinary school two months ago. He was in France and Italy for five years, but he said he wanted to come back here where he is from. He had a troubled past but has redeemed himself, and I like to give new starts in life for changed people. He is a very good chef."

"That is very kind of you, Gio. You have a wonderful heart."

"Oh, thank you, Doctor. That means so much coming from you."

"This glass of wine is wonderful."

"Would you like more?"

"No, thank you. Gio. I just have one glass a day for my health."

This has been a wonderful lunch, I think I will call it a day. I have no more appointments, and I want to go home and read my new book, Jimmy's Adventures. *It has started out so funny, and I like a good laugh, Maybe I will buy a copy for Detective Richard. He needs a good laugh, too.*

Jerri pulls up to her house screeching her tires on the circle drive. She stops at the front entrance. *Where is Jan? She usually greets me. Oh, well!*

Upon entering the house, Jerri continues musing. *I see her dogs are here, so she is not walking them.*

"Jan! Where are you?" Jerri calls.

"Oh, back here in the shed, Jerri."

"What are you doing in there?"

"Look, Sis, the bucket of sand is still glowing, and colors are moving around in there."

"Jan, have you been staring at this all day like you do the fish tank?"

"Well, yes, but no—maybe 20 minutes. It is beautiful, isn't it?"

"Come out here in the light so I can see your face."

"Okay, why?"

"Oh, Jan, you have to stop looking at the sand for a while. You are looking 15 years younger, and we will be found out."

"But, Sis, I think I am addicted to watching it, I feel so good and loved in its presence."

"I know, Jan, that is like me and the glasses, but I have to take them off to come back to the real world. You know if the Government finds out about this sand, they may take us away to who knows where and take my sand. You really look great, but now you are going to have to put makeup on to make you look older because our friends will not recognize you like this."

"Okay, Sis, but I feel so good now!"

"I know, Jan. Exposure to the silica does the same for me." She sighs. "I will probably retire to bed earlier than usual tonight."

"Why?" Jan inquires. "Did you have that bad dream again last night? I heard you at 3:15 AM again."

"Yes, and it is terrifying! It is so real. I can even smell the horse stable and hear the shouting in my ear saying, 'So you think you're too good for me, you fucking bitch? I will show you!' and then I can feel the weight on me and the feeling of being choked." She gasps and continues, "I even had a flashback to the dream during the day."

"That is really scary, and you seem to be having the nightmare more often!" Jan pauses in thought before she continues. "A story in the paper said that there have been two violent rapes in town within the last month and the town hasn't had one in the last five years. Jerri, we need to be extra cautious now. And watch our surroundings. And make sure our doors and windows are locked tight. I bought this stun gun today to keep by my bed."

"I agree, Jan, to keep this place locked up tight. So sad! Ocean Crest was so safe before the murder."

After a good, dreamless night's sleep, Jerri arrives at her office. As she attempts to unlock the glass storefront door, she spots in the door glass reflection, Chef Fabian sitting in his retired black and white police car with the markings removed he had bought from the auto auction.

He is staring at her without blinking, making the skin crawl up her back. She nervously drops her keys as she fumbles with the lock. Looking down, she hears his car door slam—oh, shit! Finally she gets her key in the lock. Quickly opening the office door, she stumbles in and slams and locks the door behind her. The office doesn't open for an hour. Jerri gazes back out the window. Fabian is standing outside his car now still staring at her. He takes a long drag off his cigarette, inhaling deeply; then he flicks the burning red cigarette butt in her direction as he walks away toward the restaurant.

Jerri is a bit shaken by this and looks for the card Richard gave her. *I may be over-reacting to this because of all the things going on, and the recurring nightmare has me all jumpy. I think it's just in my head,* Jerri reasons with herself. *I will call Jesús in for a special visit today. I want to help him so much.*

"Cassi can you call Juanita, Jesús's mom, to see if she could bring him in today?"

"Yes, Doctor," Receptionist Cassi, a young girl with blond pigtails and a bubblegum personality that really brightens the office daily, replied.

Still shaken a bit, Jerri finds Detective Richard's card and lays it by her phone. *I may call him if I get the nerve.*

Cassi buzzes Jerri's office phone. "Yes," Jerri answers,

"Juanita will bring Jesús by at 10:00."

"Thank you, Cassi." *I want to look at Fabian with these glasses, but I don't want him to see me do it.*

The time has gone by fast, and she hears a familiar little voice shout in the lobby, "Buenos dias, Cassi, where's my Doctor Jerri?"

"I am in here Jesús," Jerri shouts, "come into my big office today because I want to show you something."

"Okay, Jerri," he says as he runs in and jumps up on her lap at her computer to look at all the buttons on the keyboard. He has to squint his eyes and lean forward to see the letters.

"Jesús, you have red lips today," Jerri says. He is looking hard at a picture of her he picked up from her desk, then studying her face close, touching her nose, eye brows, and lips with his little fingers (Jerri knows he wants to remember her face image after he can no longer see) all as he is talking.

"Si, strawberries, Jerri, strawberries Papa brought home to me," he shouts with excitement! This excited little boy's talking flings spit-spray in her face. Well, that's okay with Jerri. She kisses his brown little cheeks and hugs him tight as she just sits there and smiles.

"I can always tell what's being farmed by the color of your little lips, Sweetie. Okay, now Jesús will you do something for me?"

"Si, Jerri."

"I want you to put on my special glasses for a few minutes. I know they won't fit you, but I want you to look through them for me, please will you?"

"Si!"

"Here you go. Tell me what you see as we walk outside okay?"

"Si."

Jerri puts the glasses on Jesús, and he holds them in place as he looks around the shopping center at the people walking around.

"Jerri, I see muy bien, muy bien! Jerri, what are the colors around all the people's hearts? Yellow, blue, some red, and that guy at the cop car is black, and the girl with him is brown—how nice."

"Jesús, can you see the lady walking the dog way over there by the bus?"

"Si, she has a flowered shirt, red purse, a brown and white spotted dog and yellow cloud."

"Very good, Jesús, I can't see that good. Okay, now I will remove the glasses, and you tell me what you see."

"Jerri, I see the same. The lady is picking up dog poopy now, but I don't see the colors on the hearts."

"Great! Let's go to my office and play match the shapes on the wall, okay?"

"Okay! Hey Jerri, I can find my way back in with no glasses anymore," Jesús shouts.

"Okay, Jesús, see the chart at the wall at the end of the hallway?"

"Si."

"Okay, on the line point with your finger what way the arrows are pointing. Okay, top line to the right, good. Next line down. Down is correct. Now the bottom line that is the smallest arrows. Left—perfect score without glasses."

"Doctor Jerri, me no have to wear glasses no more?"

"I believe your eye sight is repaired," Jerri says with a smile, "but I want you back here in two weeks to check them again. Okay?"

Juanita said, "I thank and praise you with all my heart, Dr. Jerri."

"You're welcome, but do not tell anyone about this. It is an experiment for my best patients, okay?"

"God bless you, Dr. Jerri."

"Thank you. There is no charge. Just go and enjoy your life!"

Jesús grabs his mother's hand and skips out to their truck. He's so handsome to Jerri now that his eyes are bright brown. *He will now live his dream to drive a truck for his own company. I'll miss his visits, but my tears are for joy.*

Now, I think I need to call Richard. Jesús saw a black cloud around Fabian's heart, and brown, that means frightened, around the girl with him. But how would I explain this cloud thing. Oh well, maybe I won't call him today. He is busy, and I don't want to over-react.

It is slow today, and there is a chick flick playing at the Ocean Crest Theater. That would be a good place to experiment with my glasses by watching the emotions of the audience as the movie plays. This will be a great test.

"Cassi, I will be leaving today. Have Dr. Shella take any walk-ins, okay?"

"Certainly, Dr Jerri."

I'll see if Jan wants to go. The start time is at 2:15 PM, so we can have lunch first and then see a movie. We haven't done that in a long time.

Jan works part-time at the Ocean Crest Veterinary Hospital for small and large animals. Dr. Jack Clark, DVM, a tall, strong, handsome, Norwegian man with thinning blond hair, runs the hospital and the only large-animal crematorium in the area. He spends a good deal of time at the Ocean Crest Equestrian Polo Club. Elegant white wood stables with red trim boards under an olive-green metal roof with cupolas—this is where the big money is, and Jan accompanies Dr. Clark because she has a natural calming effect on the horses. Dr. Clark and Carolann, his wife, are loved by the town as they used to volunteer for many charity benefits. Dr. Clark still serves in her absence, since she disappeared over four years ago, and he has also started a college tuition fund for the youth who may want to become veterinarians and apprentice with him.

Jerri pulls into her driveway and honks the horn—beep, beep. Jan steps out the back door with the curly house phone cord stretching out the door. She puts her finger to her lips to hush Jerri. She signs that she is talking, which makes Jerri lean on the horn longer as she laughs.

Jan hangs up and walks to the car saying, "I was talking to Luke. He may be my next boyfriend, but maybe not just now, Sis!"

"You like Luke? He smells like a horse stable, always wears a long sleeve cowboy shirt and hat. Yeehaw, yippy, ki-yay," Jerri teases.

"I met him at the stables on my rounds with Dr. Clark. Luke is cute for a cowboy, and his devilish crooked smile looks like he is always up to something," Jan grins.

"Yeah, I see a bright future for you with that guy. Remember the last time he took you to dinner? At the end of the meal he said it was Dutch treat and left, so you thought he was going to order a Danish for desert. Ha, ha, ha."

"What are you doing, bothering me today, Sis?"

"Do you want to go to lunch then go see that chick flick

playing at the OC Cinema?"

"Oh, yes, yes, yes! I'll get my purse!"

"Jan, we can take turns watching the people's heart colors with the Agape glasses as the movie gets sad or happy."

Both wear grins at the thought.

They walk into the Chicken Pot Pie Palace world famous restaurant; well maybe not world famous but world famous as far as you can holler world famous in this town. They serve great chicken pot pie—like homemade if you have a good cook at home.

They settle into their booth and order, and Jerri tells Jan, "I put these glasses on Jesús today, and they healed his eyesight. I am so happy. I love that little boy."

"That is wonderful, Jerri, to use glasses to heal people."

"Jan, there is something else. There is a new chef at Palermo's. His name is Fabian, and he creeps me out. His appearance is like a rockabilly. Jan, he stared at me this morning as I was trying to get into my office. The hair went up on my back, and I don't have hair on my back. Then after I locked myself in the office, he looked at me angrily and flipped his cigarette butt my direction."

"You're kidding me!"

"No, and that is not all, you know the heart cloud colors we see on people?"

Jan responded, "Yeah, green shows they feel safe, blue for stability, red mad or pain, yellow happy, brown for fear, and black for evil. Yes, I know and see, but I can tell what people are like without the glasses. I am a good reader of character."

"Well," Jerri continued, "Jesús was wearing the glasses outside the office, and he saw Fabian at his car with I guess a girlfriend, and he said Fabian has a black cloud and the girl looked scared and hers was brown according to what Jesús saw. So we have had more rapes in Ocean Crest since he showed up in town a month ago. We have to be careful. I am afraid he may follow me."

"Why don't you call your detective friend just for his opinion?" Jan asked.

"Well, maybe I can have lunch with him some time and talk about this."

Jan and Jerri enjoy their lunch, go into the theater, and settle into the perfect seats right in the middle—with the candy they sneaked in. The theater is only a third full, so there are not many people to watch with the glasses.

The lights go down and the entertainment starts with snack bar advertisement like dancing popcorn containers doing do-si-do with soda cups, a corn dog spinning a lasso to rope in the soda cup, and then cartoons and the fun stuff before the movie—a love story with lots of tears and vivid colors beaming from people's emotions viewed through the glasses.

At the end of the movie, Jan and Jerri laugh at the parts that remind them of themselves. As they walk up the aisle, Jerri wearing the glasses, laughs until she see's black and brown colored heart clouds. It is Fabian and a girl, and he gives Jerri an evil stare. Jerri pushes Jan up the ramp faster to get away from him.

"Jan! He's here!" Jerri hisses. "Let's get the hell out of here fast, do you think he followed us ?"

"I don't know. Let's go home and lock the doors."

Finally, back home all locked up for the night, Jerri says, "I am going to text Richard to see if he will meet me for lunch to talk about the rapes in town."

Jerri texts Richard, and he agrees to meet her tomorrow.

"Okay, Jan, it's all set for tomorrow."

"Good! I will feel better. That guy is so creepy." Suddenly, Jan's face goes from sober to a cheerful smile, and she shouts, "Jerri I just had a great idea for the children with special needs at the stables."

Jerri snaps her head back with surprise at Jan's enthusiasm. "What are you thinking Jan?"

"You said that the special glasses healed Jesús' eye sight, right?"

"Yes, Jan, he is healed,"

"Well, don't you see?" Jan says as she rolls her eyes up to the ceiling and back down reaching her arms out to hold Jerri's hands. " You could use the Agapé glasses to heal the children that visit the horses."

"Oh, Jan, I don't know about that. There are so many things to think about; like if the word got out that children were being healed here the town would be over run with desperate parents to have their children healed. And there might be legal ramifications." Jerri turns and leads Jan to the couch, where they sit to continue their conversation.

"Jan, I am afraid of the healing power the glasses have, and my responsibility in possesing them. The Agapé glasses are more powerful than the atomic bomb that Robert Oppenheimer with others invented during WW II, and see how that changed the world? What if someone bad got these, Jan?"

"But what about the children, Jerri? What about the children? What if they were your kids, Sis?" Jan pleads.

This emotional conversation battled on in love until late in the night, with both sisters learning to understand the other's views. Sitting on the couch, leaning on each other, they hug, and with tissues, they wipe away one another's tears. Emotionally drained, they agree to wait until they can think clearly. It has been an emotional day, and they decide to turn in.

"Good night, Jerri."

"You too, Jan. I am going to make a cup of hot cocoa with milk to help me get to sleep while I read a little more of this little book of *Jimmy's Adventures*."

They settle into bed and drift to sleep.

Chapter 3
The Visitation

A quiet night—until shadows move around in the bedroom. The clock reads 3:15 AM. Killer's hot breath moves past Jerri's ear. A hand gently strokes her long hair to the side of her face. The faint smell of horse stable fills the room. A blink of her eyes and Jerri awakes to a vision of a man's silhouette standing at the foot of her bed holding a long-handled polo mallet.

She screams, and the shadow man disappears. Her heart beats hard as she tries to catch her breath.

Jan runs into her room and flips on the light. "Did you have that bad dream again Jerri?"

"I don't think so. This was too real this time, Jan." Jerri gets up, puts on her robe, and walks down the hallway toward the kitchen. "Jan," she yells, "did you leave the front door open? It is wide open!"

"You know I wouldn't do that!" Jan hollers back as she rushes to join her sister.

Jerri slams the door shut and locks it.

Walking to the table, she sees her prescription pad is on the table with someone else's writing on it. "Jan, did you use my prescription pad to make notes?"

"No again," Jan huffs as she reaches the kitchen. "I didn't leave the door open, and I haven't touched your prescription pad, Jerri."

"I'm sure this was in my purse. Let's see what it says," she peruses the note. "This doesn't make any sense, Jan. It says 'my next visit, you will call your mother'. I don't know who could have gotten this to write on at my office, but I will find out! My guess is it was written here. So I am not going back to bed! Too keyed up to sleep. I will lock the doors myself now!"

The two women check everything as they retrace their steps to Jerri's room. "Where did this hay straw come from on my bed? Oh, this is a crazy night." Jerri grabs the bedside phone. "I am calling Detective Richard!" she says as she dials.

"I am sorry to trouble you, Detective, at this early hour."

"Who is this?" Richard's voice blurs with sleep.

"It's Dr. Jerri."

"Oh, it is late! This must be serious. How can I help you?"

"I am sorry I woke you, but I had a scare tonight. I thought someone was standing at the foot of my bed in the dark with a big handled polo mallet, and he left when I screamed."

"Jerri, lock your windows and doors," Richard sits erect, fully awake, "turn on the exterior lights, and turn off the interior ones. Give your address to me, and I will be right there. Also I have relayed this call to headquarters to request a marked car to search the area." Richard jumps from bed and partly dresses himself as he speaks.

"Thank you, Richard."

"Okay, your address please."

Jerri barely finishes saying her address when she interrupts herself. "Oh no, our power breaker must have been pulled. All the lights just went out."

"Jerri, you and Jan stick together. We are on the way." He hangs up.

"Wow! I hear sirens already, and red and blue flashing lights getting closer," Jerri yells at Jan.

"I hear a tire burnout at the back, as if a car is fleeing," Jan responds.

Jerri and Jan hug each other as they hear a hard knock on the front door with a flashlight. "Are you okay, Ma'am? It's the Ocean Crest police."

The police unit is parked next door with all the red and blue lights flashing, and neighbors look out their windows.

"Ma'am, you can turn your lights on now," the officer instructs.

"Officer," Jerri calls out the window, "the main electrical

breaker was probably shut off by the intruder."

"Officer Steve, go turn the breakers back on at the panel, but wear your gloves so you don't disturb any fingerprints."

"Okay, sir."

"Oh, hi, Detective Michaels. We didn't see anyone leave the area."

"Okay, thank you officer. I know the owner here. She called me, so I will go to the door."

"Jerri," he calls, "it's Richard. The officer says he has the breaker back on and the lights restored."

Jerri unlocks the front door and invites Richard in as Jan turns on the lights. Jerri points to the dining table with her shaking hand and says, "Please sit down, and I will start a pot of coffee."

"Are you sure you want coffee, Jerri? You look pretty shook up, but that's natural under the circumstances. I will have to make a report, so can you tell me everything you remember? Jan, you might as well join us," he calls.

"Well, Richard, I went to bed around 11," starts Jerri, "but I was only dozing because the smell of something like a horse stable odor disturbed my sleep—and I thought I heard a whisper. Then my eyes snapped open, and I saw in the dark the silhouette of a man with a polo mallet with a long handle. I screamed, and I heard Jan yelling my name. Then the man was gone. Just like that! And he left the front door open wide."

"So, your doors were locked when you turned in?"

"Yes, and Richard, we keep seeing a creepy guy named Fabian in a retired police car many places. He is a chef next door to my lab and he always stares at me angrily."

"Okay. I will check this guy out. Do you remember anything descriptive about your intruder that may help us ID him?"

"No, only that he smelled like a stable," Jerri said as she studied her folded hands in her lap and shook her head.

"Detective Michaels," an officer calls, "we didn't find any

prints on the doors, windows, or breakers in the panel."

"Thanks, Guys. Good work. This looks like someone more sophisticated. He must be wearing disposable gloves.

"Anything else, Jerri?"

"Oh yes, there are hay stems on my bed. Oh, and my prescription pad was removed from my purse, and here is what it says." She gave him the evidence.

Richard picks up the pad and reads the note scribbled on it aloud, "My next visit you will call your mother." Richard pauses and his face drains of color. He stands swiftly and walks to the officers outside.

Jerri and Jan race to the window to listen to their conversation.

"Shit, guys, the bastard is back! Shit! We've got to get him this time. He's the one who killed Crystal!"

"How do you know that, Detective?"

"Because he wrote a note that only the killer would write. I will get the son of a bitch this time because I've got some leads."

The women scurry from the window to their seats at the kitchen table just in time for Richard's return.

"A unit will stay out front tonight," he says, "so if you can get some sleep go ahead and try. It's going to be a long day. Maybe you can sleep in another one of your bedrooms tonight, Jerri, because we have to tape off your master bedroom to collect evidence later. Okay?"

Jerri nods, and Richard continues, "do you have a gun to protect yourself, Jerri?"

Jerri's mouth drops open in surprise. "No, I may shoot myself."

"Oh, don't say that, Jerri!" Richard sounds stern. "Are you suicidal?" he asks in a softer tone.

"No! I just don't know how to operate a gun," Jerri smiles.

"I have a stun gun," Jan interjects.

"That's good, Jan. Okay, Jerri. With no gun, do this! If a man ever gets on you and tries to hurt you, I want you to grab his head, pull it close, and stick your thumb in his eye socket popping his eye out. This will give you a chance to live, and since you are an eye doctor, you know how. I know it's an ugly thing to do and against your ethics, but that person will kill you if you don't, and this is a proven deterrent that always works."

Now Jan's mouth drops open while Jerri sounds doubtful. "Okay, I don't know if I can sleep now anyway. Richard, I heard your conversation with your men and …"

"Stop Jerri! I will explain everything to you maybe in a couple of days over lunch if that is okay, but for now I want you gals, if you're not going to rest, to pack up your stuff, so we can hide you until we find this guy. Okay? I will have some under cover guys follow you to work because we want this guy to think it's no big deal. And we will have a couple of lady officers stay here so things look normal. Okay?"

"I'm worried; why did he choose me?"

"I don't know his motive yet. I don't have any special glasses to search the hearts of people. I wish there were such a thing! So I will use my deductive skills that God has blessed me with and pray for His guidance. Crystal used to pray this for me, but I don't know if God hears me. I am not good like Crystal was."

"Why did you say special glasses, Richard?"

"Oh, because you make glasses and would understand the reference. That's all, and it would be cool to have some like that."

Jerri starts to say something then stops.

"Jan," Richard says, "it's your turn."

"My turn?"

"Can I ask you a few questions?"

"Sure, but I heard your guys say they didn't see anyone. I heard a car burnout at the rear as you guys approached from the front."

"Okay, thanks! Do you know anyone who would want to hurt you two gals?"

"No!"

"Do you have any male friends?"

"Oh, just Luke. He's harmless. Kinda stupid. He works at the stables. I met him while I was helping Dr. Clark out there."

"How long have you known Luke?"

"Two months or so. He travels around from state to state. Sometimes he works here when he's not doing his rodeo bull riding."

"What's his last name?"

"I don't know if he had a name before Luke."

"No, I mean like a last name like Luke Smith—you know a last name like Luke Blank."

"No, I don't know his last name. He only took me to dinner once, and we never kissed either."

"So, you don't know him very well. Does he have any tattoos on his arms or anywhere?"

"I don't know. He keeps his arms covered always in his long-sleeved cowboy shirts."

"What kind of car does he drive?"

"An old dirty El Camino—kind of a rusty white color with torn seats and hay and dirt inside and in the bed. You can't wear something nice if he's driving you to dinner. Oh, I think the license plates say Wyoming."

"Good! Thank you, Jan, you have been very helpful."

Nobody gets anymore sleep, but their day begins anyway.

Jerri stares blearily at Jan and says, "I can't get back in my room to get clothes, so can I borrow something of yours?"

"Oh, yes of course, Jerri. You can wear this sparkly green dress with the tassels that I wore to the roaring twenties party," Jan laughs in an effort to break the heaviness of the situation. It works, and Jerri laughingly shakes her head at the dress. Only Jan knows how to lift her sister up.

"I don't feel the sparkle vibe today, and my patients won't appreciate the humor. I do have a shower and change of clothes at the office. I just don't want to look like a hooker walking in from my car."

"Okay, Sis, here is a sensible outfit." Jan offers Jerri a blue pants suit.

"Thanks, Jan. We have to take our bucket of sand to the lab this morning. We can't leave it here to be found."

"Okay. I will load it in your trunk."

"Good, thank you. Umm, Jan, do you think Richard is good looking?"

"Hell, yes, he is. Why? Do you think he likes me?" Jan laughs. "I know he likes you, Jerri. When he sees you, he always hums that Billy Paul song—oh I can't remember the song name. Oh, well, yes, he likes you. I can read people. I told you that. But you don't know him yet, so take time with this guy, Jerri, he may not support you and take from you like the other men in your life. I think you need to heal yourself first. He is a cop, and they have issues. It comes with the job, Sis," Jan cautions her.

"Okay, thank you, Sis," Jerri grins secretly.

"I've got to get to Dr. Clark's. We have a big day at the stables today."

"I kind of wish you didn't have to go there today, Jan, but I guess it will be okay. I've had enough stable smell. I will touch bases with you later, when we know where we will stay tonight. Okay, Jan? I am leaving now."

"Okay, see ya!"

Jerri arrives at work before anyone else. She covers the bucket of sand with a blanket from her trunk and takes it inside her office with her where she stashes it in the closet. She also removes her emergency clothing and heads for the office shower.

Jan arrives at the stables and meets Dr. Clark. "Good morning, Doctor."

"Good morning, Jan. You look like you didn't sleep well last night."

"Oh, Doctor, what a night! Someone broke into our house, and a man was standing at the foot of my sister's bed with a club, but he ran away."

"Is that so? That is really scary. Do you think you would like to take the day off to get yourself together?"

"No, I want to work to keep my mind off of it. We have to find another place to stay until they find him, but there's not much to go on."

"Sounds similar to the lady that was horribly murdered five years ago named Crystal," Clark muses. "She spent a lot of time here. She was very smart—maybe too smart, and a beautiful lady too. Her horse is over there in stall #23, Bentley." He gestures with his left arm. "Bentley's a wonderful palomino gelding quarter horse, and she was great horsewoman. My Arabian hot-blooded stallion, Aswad Jihad or Black Holy War is in stall #22 next to her horse. I miss Crystal. That was too bad." He shakes his head.

Clark takes a shaky breath and continues, "Anyway, you know I have a large house with many rooms and a house keeper. I have a bedroom for each of you, if you gals want to stay at my estate. It's lonely out there since my wife disappeared, I mean ran off, and I can keep you two safe."

"I will talk to my sister about it. She's the smart one."

"Yes, she thinks she is; oh, never mind, but don't forget to ask Jerri. You will have the full run of my mansion—the pool, spa, open bar, sauna, and I just found a great new chef in town who moonlights. He can prepare dinners for us. It's very safe at my home with all of its state of the art security and patrols."

"Thank you so much! You're the best boss!"

"You're welcome, Jan," Clark's smile didn't quite reach his eyes, but Jan was too distracted to notice.

"Hey, Jan!" Luke shouts.

"Oh, good morning, Luke. Where were you last night?"

"I had some suds at the olo club bar and then I crashed in the bunkhouse. Why?"

"Just wondered what wild cowboys do with their off time," Jan grins.

"Well, I'd like to rope you in, you hot little filly, for a big ol' smooch right on that pretty li'l red painted mouth!"

"Well, that's why I have this big knife on my belt cowboy, to cut your rope 'cause I ain't getting roped in by no cowboy that is here today then rides off tomorrow."

"I'm almost past the age where I'll be ridin' off. You're a spunky girl, I like dat!"

"I'm not really a girl, and yeah, I found out Dutch treat ain't no damn pastry! You jerk!" They laugh together.

Brianne, the stable girl who takes care of the horses and exercises them, especially Bentley her favorite horse, speaks up, "Hey Luke! You are a jerk! You shouldn't treat my friend Jan that way."

"What's it to you, Brianne?"

"She's my Mule Kick Saloon buddy, Luke, and if you bother her again, I will blister your cute little ass with my bullwhip, and you know I can!"

"Brianne, I ain't agonna hurt her. I just wanna kiss her right on that pretty little li'l mouth of hers, that's all."

The women exchange glances and grin.

* * * * *

Back at the Vision Lab, Detective Richard stops by to talk to Jerri. Cassi buzzes her office. "Detective Michaels is here to see you."

"Thank you, Cassi. Show him to my office please."

"Right this way, Detective." Cassi sashays down the hall, and Richard smiles appreciatively as he follows.

"Good morning, Jerri. I want to talk to you about your situation."

"Yeah, I do, too, Richard. What's on your mind?"

Richard settles into the chair opposite Jerri's with her desk between them. "Well, I will give you some background. The note on your pad is chilling. It points to the man who got away with killing my wife Crystal five years ago. I was on a stakeout miles away that night when it went down.

"Jerri, I married way over my station in life." Richard seems to go into muse-mode. "All of Crystal's family are stinking rich and have a fine pedigree. They attend and put on the most elaborate events with the finest things and the richest friends. All the ladies love the polo events and wear the expensive dresses with the fancy hats, holding the best glasses of wine, but not Crystal. She loved to ride and play polo because she loved the power of her horse and his thundering hooves with the wind in her face. She trained her horse and named him Bentley. He's a beautiful Palomino. I try to find time each week to ride him, as well as my own horse Tux. They like to run on the beach. That was Crystal's favorite thing to do—feel the sea spray on her face as they ran through the surf. Oh, well, that's enough of that." Richard seems to visibly shake himself away from nostalgia.

"On that horrible night at 3:15 AM—the time the grandfather clock was broken, a man entered my house somehow. He must have had a key and known how to defeat the alarm system. He went to our bedroom. Crystal was awakened, and she hit the speaker phone speed dial for 911 but hit her mother's phone number instead. Mom answered the phone as my wife was being raped and strangled. He yelled some vulgar things at her, my mother in law said, and I guess Crystal recognized him because she said, 'I know you'. That's when he crushed her skull with what is believed to be a polo mallet, but it was never found. So now you know why I am so concerned about the note."

Jerri's face paled. "Richard, I have had a recurring nightmare just like the scene you described right now. That has been going on for four and a half years. Let me guess what he said, 'So you think you're too good for me, you fucking bitch. I will show you!'"

"Jerri, that is exactly what he said!" Richard slams his hands on the arms of the chair as he jumps to his feet. "I don't understand this," he sighs as he sinks back down. "How is it that you would have this dream? Is it a warning to you from somewhere beyond our world? This may be a prophetic dream, perhaps? I never heard of such a thing.

"Whatever it is," Richard frowns and continues, "last night's incident proves that he is still out there, and I need to find him before he strikes again. If I just could have a tool that could help me see him! Oh, well." He frowns more deeply and shakes his head. Then he drops it to gaze at his service boots and rests his elbows on his knees.

"After the murder I started drinking heavily for a year to help dull the pain of her loss, but it just made me dizzy, and I woke up with the pain still in my heart. She was my life; now she is gone. After a year, on the first anniversary of her murder, I got drunk, and I yelled at God and cursed Him for allowing her to be murdered. I mean, she loved Jesus, and what good did that do her?

"So, yeah, I am mad at God. I said, 'why her?' I shouted, 'You don't know what it's like to lose someone that is so good'. I think I heard God answer me audibly—powerful like the ocean, but with love, *'Crystal is with me. Where are you in the life I gave you? I gave my Son, whom I love wholeheartedly, for your soul and He paid the price for your sin, what will you do with your life now?'*

"I woke up in the morning and I wondered if I just dreamed that or if was it real. I drank before that because it was a way to delay the grieving process. I stopped drinking and cried for her a few days, and the healing began."

Richard sat straight and pinned Jerri with a determined gaze. "Now I won't let that guy win! Well, I am still so damned angry! If I catch this guy then maybe God has answered my prayers and then I will believe, but not until then.

"Maybe, Jerri, you are the one God sent to help me find the murderer. We will see."

Jerri rebuts, "Oh, I don't know anything about criminals or much about God. Richard, I know people who go to church, and they gossip about others. I don't want to be around those people that are so damned judgmental and negative. They have said bad things about my sister and me, mostly lies, to others. I would like to moon them if I wouldn't go to jail for it!" With every word she speaks, her voice becomes more strident.

"I feel the same way, Jerri." He grins. "If my department ever gets a call like that, I will have my men stand down, so go right ahead, girl."

They share a laugh, and Richard continues, "You are a breath of fresh air to me. You are so real and true to yourself. I think we will solve this murder together—teamwork, ya' know.

"If we do solve this murder," he takes a deep breath, "I want you to accompany me on horseback to complete one thing with me. Crystal's ashes are on my fireplace mantel in a saddle bag because she always said if she died first, she wanted her ashes spread in the ocean from horse back at sunset. But I can't do that until I catch this guy and put him away!"

"I'm honored to be asked, Richard, but I don't have a horse. I have spent time with Jan at the stables from time to time. I usually tease her boss, Dr. Clark, 'til I make him a bit red-faced frustrated, but he's nice enough—for a Norwegian."

"Jerri, I have my horse Tux, and you could ride Bentley, Crystals horse, with the saddle bag. You see that will be her last ride on her horse before she is placed in the ocean to complete her wish."

"Would she have approved of me riding Bentley? I never knew Crystal."

"Of course, Jerri, you were almost murdered by the same

guy. You are the only one qualified to do this for her, so I have to protect you and catch this guy, so he can't kill you, too. Jerri, I have prayed to the God that I cursed for a break in the case or someone that would help me catch him. I believe he just answered that prayer—if He exists."

Richard sets aside nostalgia and dreams to focus on the present problem. "Now about specifics! Jerri, you and I will need to work close on this, so I would like you and Jan to move into the in-law house that is located next to my house. Both have all the security precautions. You two will have your privacy, but we will be close enough to compare notes. You will need to be watched because I believe he is watching you. My house has a long private driveway with cameras, and I will dispatch unmarked cars to patrol periodically. We need to keep a low profile."

"I have my clothes at my house in the taped off room. "Can I get them to bring to your house?" Jerri asked.

"I think we have all we need from the scene. I am relieved it was not, fortunately, a murder scene."

"Me too—glad that it wasn't a murder scene! Okay, I will tell Jan to get her things together."

"I will call and have my officers let you into your house now to collect your things, and I will give you the code for the automatic gate on my driveway. When you two arrive at this address here," he hands her a card, "you will see the big white wood ranch-style home with a wraparound covered porch on the left side at the end of the street. But you'll be following undercover officers this first trip.

"Now, Jerri, I have some things to do, so I will meet you at your house later. It will be okay for you to go there after you leave here, and I will have an officer escort one of you to my house, and the other one will follow me when you both are ready. I don't want anyone tailing you."

"Thank you, Richard, for all the trouble."

"You'll pay by assisting me," he grins.

Richard heads out, leaving Jerri's head reeling from the new information. She rests it on her arms on her desk.

Richard needs a tool, so I will make him one. I guess I will call them The Agape Spectrum glasses, but how will he respond to these? I will make them today and give them to him tonight.

* * * * *

Jan finishes work at the stables and jumps into her truck, (oh yeah, Jan drives a cool 1956 Ford step-side pickup truck with a Boss 427 cobra jet V-8 engine, and it is painted bright red with white flames on the hood, custom leather interior, 4-speed-stick shift, and the words **Quick Chick** painted on the cab doors). She starts it up, and it roars (license plate is 2FAST4U). Jan blasts off toward home to talk to Jerri.

Jerri arrives at home and is introduced to two female officers who look similar to her and Jan. They will stay in Jerri and Jan's place until the murderer is caught. Detective Richard arrives at the home to share the plan for the move to his guest house. Jan arrives in Quick Chick.

"Okay, gals, the plan is that you two drive your own vehicles to my house using separate routes. You will both be escorted by undercover units; in fact all your protection and patrols will be undercover units from now on. We do not want the murderer to know you are being watched."

"Thank you, Richard. We'll get our things now," Jerri said.

"I'll call my boss, Dr. Clark," Jan says. "He offered us a place to stay, so I will tell him Richard is taking care of us. He was really worried for us. What a nice man!"

"Will you two ladies feed my fish?" Jan asks the officers as she hands them a metal container. "Just two pinches of this once a day."

"Oh, yes ma'am we will take good care of this place for

you."

"Okay, are you ready, ladies?"

"Yes, Sir," Jerri and Jan chorus.

"Jerri, you follow me, and Jan you follow Officer Steve. Okay?"

"No problem, Richard. Officer Steve is quite handsome," Jan giggles.

Richard shakes his head and rolls his eyes. "Okay, let's roll!"

Chapter 4
The Safe Place

The drive is uneventful for everyone, and individually, spaced many minutes apart, they wend through the automatic gate and take the driveway made of pavers and gravel almost two football fields long. It ends around the back of the ranch style houses at a six-car garage.

Richard stands beside his vehicle until Jerri and Jan both arrive and the other escort departs after leaving Jan's luggage beside Richard's car.

"All right, ladies, to your left is the guest house. I hope you will be comfortable there. It is not what you are used to having. It's only 2,000 square feet next to the 6,000 square foot main house to your right, but you can make yourselves at home there. Grace is the maid's name, and she is an excellent cook also."

"What a very impressive estate this is! You must be paid well. Oh," Jerri slaps a hand over her mouth. "Pardon me. That is none of my business."

Richard laughs. "Jerri. It's not the first time I have heard that statement, but that's quite all right. I would ask the same thing if it were someone else. Let's grab your stuff and go into the guest house."

Sharing the labor, they only have to make one trip into the house that will be home for the two women for a time.

Jerri gasps as they pass a large picture window. "Oh, what beautiful landscaping! Those lawns are huge, and I love the roses around the pergolas in the scattered pines."

Jan and Richard join her at the window. Richard points and says, "See the full-size cross that is placed in front of the bench with an engraved stone at the base? Crystal designed all of this—everything you admire. She loved to have coffee or tea in quiet places in the garden to read her Bible and pray. I asked her why she wanted this religious cross symbol. She said that it is just a reminder that He took our place on the cross. She placed a stone at the foot of the cross with John 3:16 engraved on it.

"Crystal always said, 'I don't have a religion, Richard. God hates religion. I have a relationship with Jesus, and the Holy Spirit lives in my heart. Jesus said we should believe, obey, and abide in Him, and share the good news with others. That is all there is to it.' That's what she told me."

Jerri and Jan exchange mystified glances before they return their gazes to the beautiful view outside.

"I argued with her. I said people are generally good, and she showed me in the Bible a verse that God said about us '*The heart is deceitful above all things, and desperately wicked, who can know it?*' *(Jer. 17.9)* And in another place it says, '*There is none good but one, that is God!*' *(Mat. 16: 19:17 and Mark 10:18).*

"I saw the love that was in her, but I just think if God loves us why do I see and experience so much pain in this world, ya' know? I haven't made any decision yet about my own relationship with God. I am still mad at Him. Crystal always showed me in the Bible the answer. She said we are born of Adam under sin. We are sinners from the beginning. God won't interfere with our free will. We will be judged for our choices unless we become born again, whatever that means." He draws a deep breath.

"Okay, where was I? Oh, see, the back-yard ends at the polo field."

Jerri excitedly interrupts, "And look! You can see the beautiful blue Pacific out past the polo field. What a marvelous view!"

"Yes, it is," Richard agrees. "Sometimes during her practices, Crystal would ride Bentley up to the back porch and get refreshments.

"This was all Crystal's money that she had before we were married, and so she built this house with me. Her side of the family is very rich, but you would never know that. They have a love for everyone, and they accepted me right into the family like a son. I still do my holidays with them. They are family, and they never judged me no matter how bad I got. My in-laws, Stan and Betty, would just hug me and smile and say 'if you need anything just ask. We love you son.'

"How about that? Who can love like that? Crystal did, so maybe it's their faith. I don't know. Oh, well, now you know how I have a house like this, and you're right. I could never afford it on my own."

Richard wipes a few tears off his cheeks, and all three take a few quiet moments to enjoy the refreshing view and let the peace of the scene wash over them.

"One thing I miss more than anything," Richard breaks the silence softly, "Crystal had learned sign language to witness to the deaf about the Gospel. She teased me that I didn't hear what she said to me, so each morning she would sign to me, 'I love Jesus, and I love you, and for now I am with you.' Sorry for the tears. Oh boy, that's tough. I miss that the most."

Richard wipes his damp cheeks and tries to smile. "Okay, you are my guests, so make yourselves at home. I'll show you the rest of the house." He turns, and they follow.

"What beautiful ranch style furnishings!" Jerri sighs.

"Yeah," breathes Jan. "Leather couch, polo mallets on the wall, and... Look at this picture on the mantel, Jerri. It's my boss, Dr. Clark, with Carolann his wife and Richard with Crystal, isn't it?" She glances at Richard.

"Well, yes, Jan," Richard answers. "Carolann and Crystal were best of friends just like Ethel and Lucy on that TV show. They were best friends even as children. Carolann's parents are wealthy too, so they did everything together, and Carolann would come over and take care of our pets when we were out of town. It's sad that they are both gone now." He takes a deep breath.

"And I don't see Jack, that's Dr. Clark to you gals, much anymore either." He turns and leads them toward their bedrooms as he continues, "Jack doesn't want to talk about anything anymore. He went to Haiti about five and a half years ago to check out a new drug that would sedate animals. He said he had to participate in some ritual Voodoo shit. I don't know; he seemed different, kinda' preoccupied, after that. Carolann told Crystal it was like he was talking to ghosts in his head. Jack and I used to talk a lot, but not so now—I feel the pain of missing the old times.

"I don't know why four years ago Carolann left town. She emptied their largest bank account and just disappeared to never be found. Maybe it was the loss of her best friend the year before. I guess we just don't really know people at all do we?"

He gestured to two bedrooms across the hall from each other. "These are your rooms. If you'd rather share a room, you can do that, too, but these two are at your disposal. I had to hire a maid to care for this place after Crystal died. Its too much for me."

He turned at the sound of footsteps behind them. "Oh, here's Grace now. Grace, could you show the ladies how to operate the TV and Wi-Fi and cook them up something? I have to go back out for a while, so you ladies enjoy and relax in your two master suites where you'll find fresh linen and robes. We will talk more tomorrow, okay?"

"Thank you so much, Richard," Jerri smiles shyly. "You are treating me like a queen."

"Yes, Queen Jerri, with a spear, right?" Richard grins.

"What are you guys talking about?" Jan looks quizzical.

"Well, Jan, according to Richard, my name means ruler with spear," Jerri replies with a superior smirk.

"Well, what's my name mean? My name has to mean something too!"

"Yes, Jan, your name does have a beautiful meaning. In the Hebrew Jan means 'gift from God', so you have a wonderful name," Richard says with a smile.

Jan smiles big and says, "I always told everyone that I

was a gift from God."

"Oh, yes. and that's what got you in trouble with your friends at school, didn't it?"

"Well, those girls just didn't accept the fact that I am special and so much more gifted than them, so I made them eat grass as I held their head to the ground until they admitted it. So feeding them a grass salad always made the girls much smarter." Jan laughs.

"Okay, Jerri," Richard interrupts, "I have to go. If you get frightened call me. The office in this house also has a monitor of the exterior cameras, so if you hear something, go check the monitors. They are also infrared, so you can see the heat signatures of bodies. The cameras will alert us if there is movement in the yard, but sometimes it's a deer, bobcat, mountain lion, or coyote. The system will record that, too. Okay, I am leaving now. I will see you tomorrow. You are safe here."

"Okay, Richard, see you in the morning," Jerri says. Then turning to Jan she adds, "Well, Sis, this guesthouse isn't as big as our place, but it's every bit as nice. Hope it's as safe as Richard says, but that's quite a list of critters that roam around here.

"Hope they're not as hungry as I am," Jan says as she rubs her stomach.

"Would you ladies like spaghetti with meatballs?" Grace interjects and notices her guests eager nods. "I made it fresh today for Mr. Richard, and there is plenty with toasted garlic bread. Here is a bottle of the best wine. I will pour, and you just relax."

"You are wonderful Grace. That would be a lovely way to end this stressful day," Jerri says, and Jan nods.

"Make yourselves at home, and I will bring your dinner right over."

While they wait, they walk down the wide halls, talk about how they could get used to having a maid, and admire the wonderful oil paintings on the walls of polo matches, country settings, and women dressed in fancy dresses with big flowery hats.

"All the paintings are signed at the bottom by Crystal Michaels. Wow! She had many talents," enthuses Jan.

"Yes," Jerri agrees, "this home is so filled with her love that even in her absence it fills the air."

Jan and Jerri finish their dinner and go to their separate suites to draw their baths, relax, and put an end to this day.

* * * * *

Richard arrives at headquarters and checks background searches of Fabian and Luke. Both have had lives of minor scrapes, bar fights, drunk and disorderly. Fabian also has a domestic abuse background to several women in the past but not in the last five years. It seems Fabian would snap if he thought a woman disrespected him.

These guys don't change, I'm going to put a tail on this guy.

* * * * *

It is dark, and Jerri suddenly has the creepy feeling of being watched.

"Jan I am going to step outside and look around I think someone is watching me." Before Jan can react, Jerri steps out front and looks down the driveway toward the street.

"Hey Jan!" Jerri stage-whispers, "look at that car at the end of the driveway. It's a black and white cop car! I see the glow of a cigarette in that guys shadow.

"Jerri come back in here! Why don't you use the monitor? Richard said no black and white car would come here, remember? Ours are all unmarked."

Just as she said that, the shadowy figure flicked the red glowing cigarette butt in their direction, got in the car and sped off. "Call Richard! He has found us."

Richard answers his cell phone, "Hi, Jerri, what's up?"

"Richard, I think Fabian was just here at the end of your driveway outside the gate. I saw a black and white police car and the shadow of a man. He flicked his cigarette butt at me just like

Fabian did at my office the other morning. Don't know if I mentioned that to you.

"I don't remember doing anything to him. I just inquired about him with his boss, Gio."

"You are right to call. We have no marked cars in that area, I am dispatching some now with an APB look out for any cars meeting that description. I will send a unit by his house. I will be there real soon." The line goes dead.

"Jan I am scared; how did he find us?"

"I don't know, but that is so creepy."

Richard arrives back at the house and charges in. "Are you gals okay? I see you're a little shaken up."

"I don't know, Richard; how did he find us so fast?"

"I did a back-ground check on him, and it doesn't look so good. But he hasn't done anything recently. Are you sure it was him?"

"I don't know. Maybe I am just jumpy."

"Well, that's understandable, but you are safe now. I am home, and a unit is positioned out front tonight. Okay?"

"Yes, thanks. I think I will have a clear head in the morning, but I also think we really need to talk tonight."

"I agree," Richard nods.

Chapter 5
Secrets Shared

"Jerri, were you wearing your driving glasses when you saw this guy tonight?" They sit across from each other at the kitchen table.

"No, but about that, Richard, I have something to share with you. I don't know how you will react. You may think I am crazy."

"Jerri, I know your quirkiness, and I adore that, so just how crazy is this news you are holding secret?" He grins.

"Pretty crazy, Richard. I do not need glasses any more, I have made a discovery that is mind-blowing and unbelievable, and I can't explain it. But I can see everything clearly, including people's feelings and the things of their heart."

"Well, maybe I will take that back about crazy if you truly believe this, Jerri."

"I knew you wouldn't believe me, so I brought you something to prove it! Last Friday when I was at the beach at my secret spot I took a walk up a stream bed. As I was walking, I saw a flash of light, and then, about 100 feet in front of me, I saw an aura of light and rainbow sparkles up and down the stream bank."

"You're kidding me, right? Did you have a fall lately?" Richard asked with a worried smile.

"No, Richard. It is real. I witnessed it," Jan shouts from the living room.

"Okay, Richard let me finish," Jerri continues, "as I approached the area, I discovered a pile of perfectly clear silica sand that had been energized by something that I don't know or understand. But I thought I would make some glasses from this material just to see what I would get. So Monday I made a pair of glasses and put them on, and well... I can't explain what happened. You have to experience it yourself like, Jan and I, so I made you a pair in hopes that it may help you find this guy you're hunting.

"Remember, you said the other day that you don't have glasses to see what is in a person's heart, and I asked why you said that?"

"Yes, I remember that, but what are you getting at Jerri?"

"I made this pair for you, Richard. I will tell you after you put these on for a few minutes that you will not need glasses anymore. You will be able to see… Well, here, just put these on. Then you will understand."

Jan rushes laughingly into the kitchen. "I've got to see this!" she exclaimed.

"Okay, I will put these ugly things on to indulge you, so here goes nothing… Whoa, what the? Oh, I feel so much love and compassion, what are these heart colors? "

"I will explain, Richard. So do you think I am crazy now?"

"Yes! You're a crazy genius!" Richard shouts. "What the hell are these, Jerri?"

"Like I said, Richard, I believe that maybe, well this may sound crazy but…"

"No, No, No! I believe nothing would be crazy in what you may say next."

"I don't know, but maybe one of God's angel's toes touched the sand, energizing it with Gods power. But that cannot be proven scientifically. I went to my desk and opened up a book that I remembered in college that spoke of a spectrum of light that may open up a window to God's heart, but that was just a theory. I dusted the book off and opened it up.

"The table of contents has a chapter called 'The Agape Spectrum—a Window to God's Love'. The book states that it is believed that if the particular spectrum of invisible light could be made visible somehow, it would open up the Agape Spectrum to what is God's love, and God is light, too.

"I read this and looked at the glasses, watching the energized colors moving through the lenses and wondered to myself,

Did I find the substance to make visible the invisible light spectrum that has power to see people's hearts with compassion and love beyond our human capacity? So, there you have the story. This is all just by accident."

"Jerri, wow! I believe you answered my prayers even though I don't think I really know God. Maybe He is answering my prayers by bringing a quirky scientist into my life for both of us. We now, together, will find this guy. I know it now using these glasses."

"Yes, Richard, but you need to remove them now because …"

"I am looking at your heart cloud, Jerri. Yours is slightly brownish, and Jan's is yellow.

"Yes, Richard, but take them off and look at yourself, "You can only wear them for small bits of time."

"Oh, I can see perfectly with them off."

"Yes, but now the mirror Richard. Look in the mirror."

"Wow! I look younger!"

"That's why you have to take them off. Another thing you will see and feel is that all the people you look at, you will see the sadness in their hearts, and it can be unbearable for a man to handle this much pain of all the people.

"So, you know this has to stay secret, right?" She hopes he'll agree to secrecy.

"Oh, yes! Absolutely, and who would believe it anyway? Wow! 'The Agape Spectrum'! What a great way to end the day! Okay, good night ladies. I really need to get some rest tonight, so I will turn in."

"Good night, Richard," both women echo.

"Well, he took that really well, huh, Jan?"

"Good thing for us, right?"

"Yeah," Jerri yawns. "But I am exhausted. I think I can sleep now. After the wine and the excitement of telling Richard about Agape, I am relaxed."

"Okay, but I have some friends to meet tonight at the Mule Kick Saloon so I will call a taxi to get me."

"Do you really think it's a good idea to go out?" Jerri chides, but Jan only shrugs.

* * * * *

Down at the police station there is some radio activity.

Officer: "This is unit #12 following a vehicle on Highway 40 just past Presidio that matches the description of the black and white car that was in the area where Detective Michaels put out the APB."

Dispatch: "Do you have cause to make a stop on that vehicle?"

Officer: "Yes, he is driving ten mph over the limit."

Richard, in his bedroom, listens to his police scanner and hears about the stop. He breaks into the radio talk. "Officer, go ahead and make the stop, but wait for back up before you approach the vehicle, I will be right there."

Officer: "Is this suspect dangerous?"

Detective Richard: "Just take caution, Officer!"

Officer: "Okay, I just lit him up, and he is yielding."

Detective Richard: "Great! I will be right there."

Other officers arrive, and they make their approach cautiously. The car is lit up with spot lights as they approach.

"Turn the vehicle off please," comes through the bullhorn.

The first officer approaches the car. "Let me see your license, registration, and proof of insurance and don't make any fast moves," the officer says with his hand on his service weapon.

"I won't, but why did you stop me?" Fabian asks.

"I paced you at ten miles over the posted speed limit… I will be right back," and the officer returns to his unit to run the info on the driver.

Richard arrives. "Officer, I am going to ask him a few questions while you run his info."

"Okay, Detective."

Richard approaches the car. "Mr. Spadazzi, please step out of the car!"

"Why? Am I being arrested?"

"No, you're not being arrested. "You just fit the image of a person of interest, and I just have a couple of questions for you."

Fabian climbs out of the car and holds his arms over his head.

"I did not tell you to put your hands up over your head, just relax. You act like you know the drill."

"Yes, I have been locked up before."

"Where are you coming from right now?"

"Someone left me a text on my phone from an unknown number to work an event. So I went to meet the client at 284 Rose Crest (Richard tried not to react to hearing his own address) to quote a catering job that I do on the side. I waited, had a couple of smokes, but nobody opened the damn gate. They just stared at me and then went back in the house. That pissed me off, and now you guys stop me. What the hell?"

"Take it easy," Richard says soothingly. "What is that tattoo on your right forearm?"

"That's a bird. My mom's favorite. I got that to remember her."

"Has she passed away?" Richard asked.

"Yes, five years ago, so that's why I left for Europe to become a chef—to make her proud."

Richard put on his glasses and noticed red and yellow cloud at this time not the evil black one.

"Those ugly glasses look like the ones that bitch wears at the vison place next to my work!"

"Why would you call the lady a bitch?"

"She came into my work and asked my boss a bunch of shit about me. I could hear some of it, like about my tattoos. That bitch thinks she's better than me, but I will show her someday—

you just watch!"

"Mr. Spadazzi, that sounds to me like a threat to the lady. I could arrest you for your statement."

"Yeah, but I hate those bitches that judge me for my appearance and not my cooking skills. All my life I have been put down. I took real good care of my momma when she was alive, and she always warned me about those stuck up bitches and the other ones that just want my money and want to take me away from her. They're all bitches—that's what my momma said. All of them!"

Richard noticed that the more he talked the redder his heart cloud got. He was suppressing rage inside.

"Mr. Spadazzi you seem to have an anger problem with women. We ran your background just now, and you have a domestic issue in your past."

"Yeah, but I completed anger classes like the court said, and I don't get as mad no more."

"I will ask around the businesses near your work to see if you scared any ladies, so if you have you better avoid them now since I witnessed you make a threat. I will arrest you if my office gets a complaint about you. Do you understand? You'd better be on your best behavior. Men who abuse women don't have a pleasant time in jail when the other inmates find out somehow. Do you get it now?"

"Yes, I will just do my work and be the greatest chef in this town."

"Okay, I am glad you have changed your focus. And you know you may not have heard the whole conversation by your own admission. Maybe that person was getting references to have you cater an event. Too bad! You may have blown a great opportunity for yourself."

"I didn't think about that, Detective. I will not be so defensive in the future."

The officer asked, "Detective, what do you want to do

with him?"

"Let him go. I don't have any more questions for him."

"Okay, Mr. Spadazzi, slow it down. Here's your license. Drive safe!"

"Good work, Officer Ross."

"Thank you. He didn't have any weapons in the vehicle."

"Great. You be safe tonight, and I want you to relieve the unit posted at my home tonight, okay?"

"Thank you, Sir, will do."

Well, that didn't check out. I will have to check Luke tomorrow, Richard thinks on his drive home.

Chapter 6
Mule Kick Saloon the Text

Jan calls a taxi to take her to the Mule Kick Saloon and Dance Hall.

Jerri sits up in her bed and opens her book called *Jimmy's Adventures* to lighten the mood before going to sleep. She sets her Agape glasses on a Bible on her bed stand and reads a few pages before turning out the light to sleep.

Jan is really having fun in this noisy bar with her friend Brianne from the stables. They both know how to stomp their boots. They get a lot of attention from the cowboys there because they're both lookers, too.

Dr. Clark happens to be there and dances with Jan a couple of dances, "Jan, where's Jerri tonight?" he asks as he twirls her toward him. "She could be having fun with us."

"Oh, she doesn't care much for going out late. She went to bed early tonight."

"Oh, I see, staying home all alone. That's too bad for her to miss out on the fun," he says as he twirls her away with a flourish right near the chair she's been using. "Sorry, Jan. I will see you tomorrow. I have some things to finish tonight."

"Okay, Boss, I will see you tomorrow."

At about 1:45 AM, Jan opens her purse to get taxi money, and she is flat broke. Her friends have left with their hook-ups, so she calls Jerri's phone to ask her bring her home.

As she digs for her phone, Jan says to herself, *Shit! Sis will be pissed off when she gets this call, but here goes.* Jan dials Jerri's number and she hears the ring tone "Turkey in the Straw" deep in her purse. *Oh, shit that's her ring tone for me. I accidently grabbed Jerri's phone, too. What am I going to do now?*

"Hey, Buck," she calls the bartender, "can you give me another beer on credit?"

"Hell, no, Jan! You know that. See the sign? "<u>You got no</u>

<u>Money for Beer? Then Get the Hell Out of Here"</u>!

"Okay, Buck. No hard feelings." *Hey Jerri's phone has Richard's number in it. I will call him on her phone.*

She dials Richard.

"Hi, Jerri, how can I help you?"

"Richard, it's Jan."

"Are you gals okay? I can be right there."

"Oh, yes, we're okay. I just grabbed Jerri's phone by accident, so I can't get ahold of her to bring me home from the Mule Kick, and I am out of taxi money."

"I am glad you're okay. I will be right there. It's 2:20 in the morning. I thought you'd be in bed."

"I had plans here with my friends."

"Okay, I'm on my way!" It's a good thing she couldn't see his scowling head shake.

"Thank you, Richard."

"Yeah, yeah, yeah!"

Jan is standing out front of the Mule Kick when Richard pulls in. "Okay. climb in, and let's get you home now."

"Okay, thank you so much Richard."

"I hear your phone ringing."

"That's Jerri's phone. It's a text message from unknown number. Who would text her at this time of night?"

"What's it say, Jan?"

"Oh, it's stupid. It may be from a drunk."

"What's it say?"

"Something like, 'Time to call your mom, bitch!'"

"Shit! We have to stop him right now! I will call her on the home phone while we go and intercept Luke. He's a suspect, and I haven't interviewed him yet. Where can we find him now, Jan?"

"I don't know; maybe the bunkhouse. That's where he lives."

"Okay, buckle up! We've got to catch this guy now!"

Richard screeches out of the Mule Kick Saloon parking lot and calls officer Ross posted in the street at his house as well as the officers at Jerri's estate. "You all keep a look out for any cars coming around my house and Jerri's. I believe the killer is going to strike tonight. I don't think he knows where she is yet.

"Affirmative, Detective!" the officers at all the locations reply.

Richard and Jan skid to a stop in the bunkhouse area.

"Jan, what one does he live in?"

"Number two."

"Okay, you stay here. I am going to get him."

Richard pounds on the door but there is no answer—no sound from inside.

"Shit! He's gone! We have to get to my house!"

"Richard, that's Luke stumbling back from the Polo club bar right there coming through the barn."

"Hey, Jan did you miss me?" Luke slurs his words.

"Stop right there, Mr. Greives. Put your hands over your head." Richard's temper flashes, and he slams Luke up against the stable wall, hard.

"That's not very friendly," Luke says.

"What's this in your pocket?"

"It's a tooth, Sir."

"Did you lose a tooth?"

"No, that dumb shit outside the Polo bar made a nasty remark about Jan, so I shut his damn mouth with my fist."

"Why do you have it in your pocket?"

"Shucks, it's just a souvenir that I stood up for Jan's honor, I can put it on a necklace for her if she wants. Hey, Jan you want a tooth necklace to show you that I love you?"

"Oh, Luke. you're drunk. You won't even remember this in the morning," Jan says.

"Okay, you're clean," Richard finishes his pat-down of Luke. "Where are you coming from now?"

"I just told you guys; the Polo bar, Sir!"

"Why are your arms covered up? Are you hiding something?"

"Yeah, I am hiding 'em."

"Let me see them?"

"Okay, but these are butt-ugly scars. I got 'em burned in a fire when I was a kid.

Luke frowns and interrupts himself. "Hey, Jan! I never saw that scorpion tattoo on your arm before now. I don't like tattoos. People shouldn't mess up their pretty skin, I do know about this!"

"How long have you had that tattoo?" Richard interrupts sharply.

"Back off, guys! It's not a tattoo," Jan defends herself. "Dr. Clark has removable animal tattoo stencils for the kids to put on at the office."

"Damn!" Richard explodes. "So a person without tattoos could give others the impression he has them!"

"Hey! There's his vet truck over there. He must be working tonight," Luke observes. "But his horse Aswad Jihad is gone; I noticed when I came through the barn."

"Oh, shit!" Richard yells. "It's him! He's the killer! Clark is the killer!"

A startle reflex takes Jan and Luke into each other's arms for support in light of that shocking announcement.

"Officer Steve!" Richard shouts into his radio, "The killer is Dr. Jack Clark. He is riding his horse to my house! You have to get Jerri to safety right now! You got that?"

"Yes, Sir! The lights on your property just went out."

"Damn! He's there!"

"Detective, I am running up your drive now, and I hear some...."

"Officer Ross! Officer Ross! Officer Ross! He's not answering, and the house phone is dead too." Richard runs for his vehicle frantically.

* * * * *

Tic tock, tic tock. The living room grandfather clock counts the seconds down... tic tock, tic tock... then chimes three times. A hinge squeaks slightly as her bedroom door slowly opens. The dark shadow of death slithers into Jerri's room, creeping in silence, ever so close, kneeling down at her side, his hand gently brushes her hair away from her sleeping face. The soft illumination from the full moon-glow enhances the contours of her beautiful, womanly form fully captured by his eyes. Heart pounds harder with excitement now, faster it races. His eyes wide open, his body now firm, and rigidly ready for the attack.

His warm breath whispers softly and close into her sleeping innocent ear. "All alone now my sweetheart. We are all alone now my dear. What a shame...even with this beautiful face, with complexion so clear, we now will forever put you in your place. The future you planned we will now erase. I am the last real man that your trembling body will feel. Just delighting ourselves in pleasure before we kill you for the thrill."

Jerri starts to awaken a little bit because of the stable odor and whispering. She sees the shadow of a man with a mallet standing—he has moved to the foot of her bed. *Oh, no, I am having this damn dream again. I'm going to turn on the reading light. Huh, there's no power.*

"TIME TO CALL YOUR MOM BITCH!" He screams, leaps on top of her, and tears her night gown open.

She shrieks, and he chokes her into silence with his other hand. He screeches, and as he gnashes his teeth madly in her face, spittle flies from his mouth along with many deep voices yelling "So you think you're too good for me, you fucking bitch? I will show you!"

Jerri starts to feel weak. Sleep beckons her, and then she remembers what Richard said. She feebly reaches up and grabs the ski mask.

He jerks away with a snarl, his grasp on her loosens a bit, and the mask slips off. She grabs his head with her now free left arm, brings it close, and jams her fingers behind his jaw for leverage. With her right hand she slips her thumb alongside his nose thrusting it deep past her knuckle into the eye socket, popping his left eyeball out.

He screams, "You bitch! I'm going to kill you," as he rolls off the bed to the floor blinded and swinging his arms wildly around to grab her.

Jerri grabs her Agape glasses and makes a break for it, running down the moonlit driveway screaming for Officer Ross.

It's a long driveway, 200 yards. Half way down the driveway she hears thundering horse hooves drawing close behind her; louder and louder the thundering hooves become. *I've got to reach officer Ross. Why can't he hear me?*

Dark demonic burning sensations sting Jerri's back from the evil words that are thrown from Clark's tongue, as from a whip, sending evil, invisible claws that grab, piercing her back to slow her pace. The oppressive spirit of darkness tries to break her will to live. Her spirit weakens toward breaking. The demons are too big to fight on her own.

I've got to get to officer Ross, she tells herself as the thunder sound gets closer. She leans forward to run harder. Stinging bolts of pain streak up her legs from the sharp gravel rocks piercing her tender bare feet.

So tired. Need to rest. Can't leave my grandkids now. She visualizes their little faces in her mind.

Oh my God! Please save me! Jerri subconsciously screams. Her shredded feet are sharply painful and bloody from the gravel drive, but she pushes on toward Officer Ross, thinking *he's my only chance to survive.*

She's almost to the street, but thundering hooves beat louder. She glances back. Clark is now down upon her, his fiery mad face lit by moonlight. Through her glasses, his heart cloud is not a color. It's a window into the pit of hell, flames lashing out of his chest like serpent's tongues. His eyeball hangs out of his face and slaps his cheek. The mallet spinning over his head now swings down fast to explode her brains out of her skull. Facing forward again, running with all her energy, she trips over officer Ross's body. She screams as she falls, feeling only the wind of the mallet that just misses her head.

Clark stops and turns Aswad Jihad around. He pauses with rage in his eye, ready to charge once again. Jerri's life's end is only seconds away. This time he will not miss! Time seems to slow down.

Jerri stumbles, falls; her glasses fly up in the air as she climbs back up to her bloody feet. Ross, her last hope for life is lying lifeless on the street. Jerri looks at Clark's flaming red face and knows this is how her life will end, and now. As if in slow motion, she watches her Agape glasses sail up into the air then tumble, shattering on the ground.

Suddenly, the energy flashes from the broken glasses in a vortex of spinning bright light rising up high and becoming a standing, translucent white, twelve-foot-tall Warring Angel of God with a broadsword of fire in his right hand. The angel stands between Jerri and the demon possessed man. Aswad Jihad rears, throwing Clark to the ground, where he lies, unconscious.

The sound of sirens gets closer, so Jerri stumbles down the road after passing the gate. Richard, racing up the road, sees Jerri stagger down the road toward him with her torn nightgown and bloody feet illuminated by the car's headlights. He jumps from his skidding car and races to Jerri as her arms reach out to him. She collapses into his strong arms.

Richard lifts her unconscious body and carries her toward his car—one arm under her knees, while he strokes the hair off her panicked face with the hand on the arm around her shoulders. "You're safe in my arms, Jerri. No one will hurt you now." He kisses her forehead and hugs her trembling body tighter as she regains consciousness.

"Jerri, you have blood on your feet but also your hand."

"My hand has his blood," Jerri quavers, "and it is starting to burn my skin. Death chased me tonight, Richard. Death chased me tonight, and I saw the pit of Hell in Clark's heart with my glasses. The flames of hell were like serpents' tongues lashing out from his chest."

"How on Earth did you escape this?" he places her on the hood of his car.

"I don't know. I think I screamed something without speaking, but I don't remember what now."

"Jerri, we didn't suspect Dr. Jack Clark of being a murderer. Jack's a family friend, and I know he didn't have any tattoos. I only put the pieces together at the stables after questioning Luke and seeing Jan's phony tattoo. I failed you, Jerri. I didn't protect you. I am so sorry for that."

"Richard, you did save me!"

"How?"

"You taught me to pop his eye out, and I did. That gave me time to run away. He almost strangled me in my bed, and I remembered what you said just before I blacked out. I would be dead if not for that. A normal human would have been out of the fight after losing an eye, but he has demons in him. I think he is dead over there where he fell off his horse."

"Jack Clark fell off his horse? That's hard to believe. He is a master horseman!"

"Well, you wouldn't believe what happened if I told you what saved me."

"You're probably right, and I don't think I can handle any more surprises tonight. He is caught now. It's all over. You don't have to worry anymore. Let's get your hand washed off. I have bottled water here in the car."

More police units arrive and start surrounding the property. The thundering sound of Clark's horse's hooves are heard fading in the distance. The property is so dark the galloping can be heard but the horse not seen.

"Call an ambulance, guys. Officer Ross is over there. Check him out. I hope he's not dead! And arrest Dr. Clark for the murder of Crystal and attempted murder of Jerri and Ross."

Jan arrives, having urged Luke to push his pathetic wheels to the limit, and talked her way through a battery of police officials. She comforts Jerri as only Jan can.

"Detective Richard!" an officer shouts, "He's not here!"

"Who's not here?"

"Dr. Clark!"

"What?"

"He's gone!"

Chapter 7
The Escape

The only thing the people in this small town talk about is Dr. Clark and his escape. It's been a week since his disappearance. The sound of the evening red wine glasses clinks above the intriguing speculations about the whereabouts of the fugitive, Dr. Clark, whom the town had admired greatly before the murder. And what of his wife? Did she run away or did something diabolical happen to her?

The details of Detective Richard's wife, Crystal's chilling murder are whispered in hushed bar table talks. The cold-blooded murder runs chills up their backs—colder than all of their chilled, blood-red wine bottles sitting in their racks.

Dark spirits in the night air seem to have overtaken the town. The haunting has started through Ocean Crest, and on this very night will visit someone's dreams. (Imagine invisible demons huddled in secret scheming their attack, conjuring up the fable told of chance. These spirits will choose your fate by a lucky spin. Now a pea is dropped on the roulette wheel of nightmares. What home will it be in? What home will the dream spirits strike? Well, let's just wait and listen to where the scream comes from tonight).

The dark shadow-man with a polo mallet is the spirit that flows through the night—the dream monster that a person sweats and wrestles with all through the longest night. The town hears horrific night screams through their Ocean Crest cool window screens. This dream strikes someone from the roulette spin in this town every night, and now again it's 3:15 AM—time for the chilling fright.

Conversations continue in the quaint outdoor clubs, for fear that they are the ones that will be next. They all fear that the spirits' roulette spin pea will drop on their house tonight for the visitation of the shadow demon that strikes every night.

Jerri is no longer visited by spirits, dreams, or demons.

Richard bought her a golden locket necklace that holds a mustard-seed sized grain of the Agape energized sand, and she always wears it around her neck. She wants God's presence with her, and that is the only way she knows to get it. Will she learn a better way? As she rests and heals, she refines more Agape sand into lenses, which she fit into several different frames.

The Ocean Crest district attorney has launched an investigation into the disappearance of Mrs. Carolann Clark five years ago. Detective Richard has voiced his opinion only to Jerri of his gut instinct. He believes Clark murdered his own wife because he feared she suspected he had killed Crystal. And he probably withdrew the two million dollars from their bank account himself to make it look like she left home .

The night of the attack on Jerri a week ago. Clark escaped on horseback. The hoof prints led the police down past the polo field into the stream bed. Then they disappeared into the ocean's surf. Did he ride north, or south to Mexico? It doesn't matter, because he is still at large.

There were sightings reported of a sailor with an eye patch that sailed out of Ensenada, Mexico a couple of days ago. Could it be Clark? He was captain of his own power yacht. He may have purchased a stolen sail boat in Mexico and could be heading anywhere in the world right now.

Detective Richard arrives at his office and has a message on his desk from a friend, Zeke, who has a business taking people out sport fishing in Ensenada, Mexico. Richard had contacted Zeke last week to keep an eye out (no pun intended) for a one-eyed man that may come to that city.

Richard returns the call. "Hi, Zeke; you left a message that you may have spotted a one-eyed guy in your town?"

"Hi, Richard, I'm happy to help you. Yes, I saw the guy across the dock making a cash deal on a 50-foot sail boat as I was docking my Mako power fishing boat."

"Thanks, Zeke, that has to be him."

"He was a bit dirty—torn clothes, a little blood stained, and he carried a big canvas type bag with a shoulder strap. But nobody asks questions down here if you want to live long. I watched him sail out of here yesterday, and then I contacted your office."

"Do you have any more info on this guy?"

"At the bar, I talked to the Hawaiian man, I didn't ask his name, that sold his sail boat named *Sail Away*. The words in Hawaiian are *Holo Aku*. It's a beautiful full-sized Cruiser, Beneteau Sense, 50-foot-long, sold to a one-eyed man for $300,000 cash— easy for one man to sail alone around the world.

"He said that the guy contacted him a few days ago on the underground boat broker and offered $100,000 cash over the asking price if he would deliver it down here fully stocked and ready to go. So, he did, and then the Hawaiian guy sailed out with his cash, perhaps to Hawaii, on another sail boat."

"Did he say where Clark was sailing to?"

"The Hawaiian guy said that the buyer was wanting to go someplace haunted. How crazy is that? He said that's where he wants to live, so he suggested an island named Palmyra Atoll in the Pacific."

"Thank you, my friend. I will send you some clients for your help."

"Thanks, Richard. You come too, I will help you land a big one, okay?"

"I will do that soon, Zeke. Bye, now."

Wow! I got you now, you son of a bitch! I'm going to catch you with my own bare hands. But how? Oh, I know, I'll hire Bill Boyd to help me catch this son of a bitch, since he has a racing sail boat. We can catch Clark. He won't suspect a cop on a racing sail boat 'til it's too late.

Richard picks up his phone and enters Bill's number.

"Hi, Bill, this is Detective Richard of Ocean Crest, and I am calling on official business. I need your help."

"Hi, Richard, I would be glad to help you. What do you need?"

"Bill, I am chasing a fugitive named Dr. Jack Clark, and from the info I got from an informant, he has purchased a sail boat in Ensenada, Mexico. I think it is like a 50-foot Beneteau Sense. I believe he has set sail to an island named Palmyra Atoll.

"Okay, we will catch him Richard, but I have a race to complete first. So this is the plan. I have my Santa Cruz 50' *Nui Koa*, that means *Great Warrior* in Hawaiian. My plans are to sail back to Hawaii to meet up with the fleet of sail boats off Diamond Head, then race Oahu to Tahiti. We can make that run to Hawaii in nine days. It's about 2,170 miles, but that's out off the great circle sailing route that passes by Palmyra.

"The other fleet is leaving from Point Fermin, CA in two days, racing to Point Venus on the northeast side of the main island of Tahiti.

"The boat Clark is sailing by himself can make 6-8 knots. Once he hits the doldrums, which run between five degrees north and five degrees south of the Equator, he'll slow down to 2-3 knots. This will put him into Palmyra in 24-26 days. If we join the fleet racing from Point Fermin, the distance is about 4,250 miles. We would be sailing with a full racing crew, with our spinnaker up, we'll be surfing off at speeds up to 24 knots, this is three times faster than what his vessel is cruising. We could finish the race in 16-18 days, drop off the racing crew, and sail back up to Palmyra to be there before he arrives."

"You are the best, Bill. I am bringing Jerri with me also. We will meet you tomorrow at the boat in Long Beach."

The minute Richard hangs up, he calls Jerri to tell her the news. "Good morning, Jerri, I've got great news!"

"Good morning to you too, Richard. I am having my coffee. What is the great news?"

"I just found that son of a bitch!"

Jerri sprays her coffee from her mouth, "What?"

"I know where he is."

"Do you have your men on the way to arrest him?"

"Well, no, Jerri, here's the thing—he bought a 50-foot sailing vessel in Mexico and has set sail for a haunted island called Palmyra in the south Pacific."

"Is the Coast Guard going after him?"

"No, he is probably in international waters now, and I want to catch him with my own hands." He paused, "And Jerri I want you to be there with me."

Jerri carefully set down her coffee mug. She took a big breath and released it. "Why do you need me?"

"Jerri, you can I.D. him, and I want you to have the memory of him being put away, so your nightmares will be put to a stop."

"Wow! I don't know, Richard, how are we going to catch him?"

"Here's the plan. My friend, Bill Boyd, is a captain of a racing sailing vessel, and he is starting the race. We will board his vessel in Long Beach and sail to Hawaii, race to Tahiti to finish the race, drop off the crew, and sail to Palmyra—beating Clark to the island. He will not suspect us of being there, and that's when I will arrest him."

"Okay, I guess, if you're sure I'm necessary to the trip, but I will have to figure out what to wear."

"Suggestion; no high heels please." Richard laughs.

Jerri sees no humor, or even sanity, in the plan. "Very funny! I'm still wearing slippers most of the time!"

"Are your feet healing? Can you fit them into tennies? You have to get ready. We are leaving tomorrow. Don't forget your locket. I believe it will protect you."

"Don't worry, Richard. My feet will probably survive, and I never take off the necklace!" Reluctantly she shudders, "Okay, Richard, I will prepare for the trip."

"Oh, Jerri, I am so busy, but I would like to ask a favor of

Jan from now until we return."

"Okaaay, what is it?"

"Do you think she would exercise my horses?"

"I believe she would love to, but I will ask," she sighs in relief. "I will call her now."

They say their goodbyes and hang up.

"Hi, Sis, what's up?" Jan chirps.

"Richard wants me to ask if you would do a favor for him."

"Okay, what is it?"

"He is so busy now, and will be for a while, so he would like to know if you would exercise his horses for him."

"Oh, yes! I would love to do that! And with Brianne! We will take them to the ocean to let them run in the surf. She loves Bentley so much. He is smart and funny, and he smiles!

"Besides, Luke is good with horses. He can shoe them, and also he called his rodeo vet friend in to take over the horses' care down here at the club. I helped him today, and he is very good with the animals. Rocky is his rodeo clown name, but Dr. Stanton, DVM, is his professional name."

"So, you like Luke, do ya?" Jerri teased.

"Yes, I saw him the other day working with some disabled children at the stables. He gave them horse rides and acted funny, made faces to make them laugh. When they left (he didn't see me watch him) he went behind the hay barn and cried for the children and tried to hide wiping his tears with his shirt sleeves. I think he has a bond with them because I think he might have been teased as a child. I don't know, but there is something he ain't telling. I heard him say to himself, 'I'm gonna miss them li'l ones. I wish I could fix 'em.'

"See Jerri, that is his heart. I said I don't need those Agape glasses to see people's hearts," Jan said. "Oh, he's a smart ass, I will give you that, and he is simple, hardworking, hard living, and battle scarred from the bull riding, but he is a good man

Jerri. He's a good man."

"Jan, are you gonna' rope him in now?" Jerri's smile is even heard in her voice.

"I reckon I will, Jerri, I reckon I will. Maybe I will at least give him that big ol' smooch on the face he wanted! Okay, Sis, I have to go help Dr. Stanton. He and I are performing by using FLIR Thermal Imaging for Equine Thermography today checking for injuries on the polo horses before the event. We can find ligaments or joints that are showing hot areas that are not visible to the eye. Hey, that's kinda like the Agape glasses, huh?"

"Yes, that is a different light spectrum also. Okay, have fun today!" Jerri concludes the call. *Well, now, I can sleep in peace knowing the whereabouts of Clark. Wonder if that will carry over into the trip.*

* * * * *

Jan covers her truck at the stables. It's kinda dusty there, and she keeps a clean machine—unlike Luke with his rust bucket, but that suits his needs.

"Good morning, Sally," Jan greats the stable dog, a blue-eyed Australian shepherd that someone dumped at the stables four years ago as a pup, and everyone adopted her as the official stable dog. She is so smart, and all the horses love her. She even gets along with the barn cats that keep the rodent population down. Sally mothers the kittens. She likes to lick them. Sally helps Jan, too. Jan can give Sally the reins, and Sally will walk the horses to the wash area or anywhere Jan tells her.

Oh, good; here's my buddy, Brianne.

Brianne comes down the driveway fast in her brand new, jacked up 4 X 4 Chevy diesel pickup truck.

I gotta ask her about riding Bentley for Richard.

Brianne hops down from her truck and starts to say hi to Jan, but Dr. Stanton yells at the women, "Hey, girls, let's go to the Polo Club for lunch now. I am buying. I don't like to eat alone, and we can talk strategy on how to do the best job for the club."

Jan and Brianne look at each other, shrug their shoulders and say, "Cool! Let's go get lunch."

Dr. Stanton says that he will stay on to run the animal hospital until a replacement is found. It seems that Clark is only one in a partnership of three that is invested in the hospital.

After lunch Jan and Brianne saddle up the horses to exercise them along the beach.

Brianne says, "Follow me, Jan, down the stream bed," so they make their way down to the surf. Sally follows them. She likes to run. Brianne takes off north up the beach running Bentley in the shallow surf. The spray fills the air, and the wind cools their faces, as the nostrils of the horses flare for better inhalation, making power for their legs. They gallop up the beach a couple of miles until they come to a big California oak tree in an area with some grass.

"Hey, Jan, let's stop and talk a bit under this tree."

"Okay, sounds good, looks good."

They tie the horses to the tree and sit down on the grass patches that are between the sandy areas, Sally runs up to the women and licks their faces, and they laugh and pet her."

Jan asks, "Sally, do you want some girl talk?"

Sally barks, and then she runs around smelling the area.

"How is Jerri doing, Jan?" Brianne asks.

"Well, her feet are healing from the cuts, but she is very jumpy."

"I can understand that. Have they got any leads on Clark yet?"

"I haven't heard anything, so we don't know if he will try again. Ya' know he is demon possessed."

"That is so scary!"

Jan continues, "Jerri doesn't feel safe anywhere. She was attacked while we stayed at Detective Richard's place, and she couldn't stand the thought of sleeping in that bed again. So we moved back home." She muses and adds, "I don't think either of us ever really relaxes any more."

Chapter 8
Sally's Treasure

"Hey, Sally, what are you digging over there?" Jan asks. "It sounds like you're scratching something hard."

"Let's go see," suggests Brianne.

"Oh, Sally, stop digging! Looks like the sand here has been disturbed recently. What is this big plastic container?" Jan wonders aloud. She removes more sand with Sally's help and wipes the sand off the cover lid with her hand.

"Brianne," Jan yells, "listen to what the lid says, "472-MED-AMB 7'X 3' Medical Supply Container; property of DVM, Jack Clark."

Jan queried her thoughts, "What is this doing here, Brianne? Let's open it!"

They unhook the latches around the lid and lift, breaking the airtight seal. Jan peeks inside, "Looks like a sweatshirt, ski mask and..."

Brianne interrupts shouting, "That's a Polo club there and it looks like it's blood stained with hair on the mallet head!"

"I'm calling Richard. We can't touch anything. Get back, Sally, but you're a good dog for finding this. Let's lay the lid back on it."

Jan calls, "Richard, we have found something like a chest buried under an oak tree about two miles north of the stream bed. Sally, the stable dog, dug it up here."

"Be more specific. What kind of chest did you find?"

"It's a heavy plastic medical chest with Dr. Clark's name on it. There's a lot of stuff in it, including what appears to be a bloody polo mallet."

"Okay, don't disturb anything, or did you two already compromise the area?"

"Jan!" Richard sounded forceful when Jan didn't answer.

"We took the lid off, but we only looked at the stuff inside. We didn't touch any of that."

Richard sighs, "Well, it could be worse. Good job. I will be right there."

Richard arrives with the police 4 X 4 units including a team to secure the site.

He strides to the women. "Okay, where is it?"

"Right there under the tree," Jan points, "and it looks like someone was here not too long ago. The soil was loose before Sally started digging."

"Okay, men, let's tape this area off." He glances into the chest. "Yes, that could be the murder weapon. The discoloration on it could be blood, and, oh, man this is hard to look at, the hair stuck to it is the same color as Crystal's. Let's hope this will connect him to her murder. Also looks like a ski mask and a bloody sweat shirt, too. Okay, guys, get all this to the lab, pronto."

He turns to the women. "Thanks, gals, and you too, Sally. Come here and let me pet you. You deserve a big steak, girl. I would say this stands for a celebration, but how do you celebrate finding a possible murder weapon of your wife?

"Jan, you three girls found the weapon, and there is a reward for any evidence leading to the arrest of the murderer. It was put up by the wealthy friends of Crystal's parents. It is $1,000,000 that you two, (and the dog?) will be splitting."

Brianne and Jan look at each other and hug and jump a little.

Brianne says, "This will change my life, Jan!"

"I know. My sis is the rich one, but she loves me. Okay, let's go back to the stable."

"Hey, Jan, you tell your sister what you gals found, okay? You deserve to surprise her this time," Richard says. "Jan, you call, and I will meet you two at the Mule Kick in one hour, and it's on me.

"By the way, Jan, I told Jerri that I located Clark, but we have to sail to the Equatorial Northern Pacific to arrest him."

"Richard, that's great news!" Jan pauses and frowns. "At least I think it is. How is Jerri taking it?"

Richard hesitates. "I don't think she's too keen on the trip, but she's game."

"Trip? What trip?"

"Jerri and I will be leaving tomorrow to sail a race that ends in Tahiti and then to the island where Clark is going."

"My sister's doing that? Why? What did you do to her?"

"Okay, we will talk later." Richard shakes his head. "See you at the Mule Kick this evening."

"Okay! Let's get the horses back to the stable, now."

Brianne and Jan gallop off with Sally running along.

* * * * *

Later, down at the Mule Kick Saloon, Richard, Jan and Brianne arrive and order a pitcher of draft to be brought to their table. They are just starting a conversation when Luke walks in.

"Hey! Jan, ya wanna dance? I'll put something on the jukebox."

"Okay, big cowboy, show me what you got!"

Luke picked a Vince Gill song, "What the Cowgirls Do."

Luke bows to Jan and takes her hand. They waltz and swing and twirl all around that dance floor.

Richard asks Brianne for the honor of a dance, and because she ain't gonna be outdone by Jan, she accepts. And here they all go tearing up the dance floor—spinning, flipping—it's a competition now. These couples are twirling around each other, moving to the music until the song comes to an end.

Whew, they're all sweaty now. That's okay. They all smell like horses anyway, except Richard.

They all settle back at the table and Richard asked Luke, "What are your life plans, Luke?"

"I don't know. I just play it by ear. I go job to job. I wanted to win the big one in bull riding, but I'm getting too old for that game." He shrugs, "But I follow the circuit anyway."

"So, you don't see settling down somewhere in your future?"

"Nah! I don't have a reason to stay anywhere. I got no family."

"Would a good woman help you to change your mind to settle down?"

"Where can you find one of those?"

"You've got two good ones right here at this table, you jerk!" Brianne shouts.

"I'm kidding!" Luke defends himself, "but I can't keep a regular job, I have to be around horses or I ain't happy."

"Why don't you do something with disabled children at the stables?" Brianne asked. "I saw you with them, and you are a natural with the kids."

"I would love to do that."

"What stops you?" put in Jan.

"I don't have money, and I can't make a living doing it. I do have a heart for them, though. I guess maybe it's because I had my arms burned in a fire as a child."

"Can I ask how?" Jan and Brianne speak together as Richard motions for the waitress to bring them new beers.

Chapter 9
Joey and Sarah

"I don't like to talk about it," Luke takes a big breath and a small sip of his drink, "but okay, here goes. I was five years old, and we lived in a small two-bedroom, wood-sided house with white peeling paint in Wyoming—my dad, mom, me, and my baby brother Joey.

"We were poor. Our house was on the ranch property where my dad worked. I kinda was with Dad a lot in his old pickup truck, running down the ranch dirt roads, kicking up dust. I remember bouncing on the truck's spring seats. We would fix the fences. I can remember it so well, like it's now. I can even smell the fields—and also the cow shit. I'd have to watch my step or get laughed at by Dad.

"I think of riding in this noisy, rattling, old truck looking at my daddy driving, with a hay straw hanging out of his mouth, with his sweat stained cowboy hat. We roll up the dirt drive. I see Mom is hanging clothes on the line out back to dry, with brother Joey in a basket.

"Oh, damn, look at him. He's got a damn blue bow that she put on his head. What the hell is up with dat? He looks stupid. He's a boy. He's my brother. My brother ain't no damn doll!"

Richard stretches his legs under the table, and all three in Luke's audience laugh.

"The yard has big shade trees, a garden, a wraparound covered wood plank porch that we sit on after supper, and Dad rocks in his chair and tells us stories while smoking his sweet tobacco pipe 'til the sun goes down. Mom made us pie today from berries, or sometimes the apple or peach trees. Boy, what a treat! I can tell you this like it is right now because I just lived it again. I have my family here with me right now in my mind.

"This all ended one night. Joey was bedded in his crib in

my room by the door. They said it was a lamp cord spark that lit the living room drapes on fire. My door was closed. It was maybe midnight or so. I woke to smoke and an orange and red glow around the cracks in my bedroom door. I remember the smoke was so choking. Joey and I screamed for our mom and dad, but nothing happened. The smoke was so thick now, I opened the window, and a fireball blew open my bedroom door. The fireball blasted into the room. *I have to get Joey. He stopped crying.* I battle the smoke, and the flames are burning me—fire so hot, *but Joey! I got to get him.* I pull him out the window with me and carry him to the end of the yard. Joey isn't breathing. I try to shake him real good, but, hell, I can't fix my li'l brother. I want him to cry, but he don't. I shake and yell in his face, but he is limp. I hug him hard." Luke gasped for breath.

"Jan, I'm so sorry I'm starting to cry now. It's so hard to live this all again," Luke gulps as his heart breaks, tears welling up in his eyes and running down his cheeks. His bottom lip quivering, Luke hangs his head and rubs his eyes.

Jan and Brianne, both in tears themselves, lean across the corners of the table and hug Luke as he shakes and sobs. "Luke you don't have to say any more," Jan pats his back comfortingly.

"No. that's okay gals, I have to finish. I haven't ever told anyone before now. I never had a friend before. I ain't easy to get to know. Had one girlfriend once, but that was just a wicked game. I don't trust people. I trust my horse, and that's all. So this memory, it's been buried inside me so long now, maybe that's why I have a death wish living a hard life riding bulls. I always think *why wasn't it me?* Why Joey, and not me?

"I sit at the tree. I hold my li'l brother in my lap. His li'l face looks peaceful enough even covered in black soot. My arms have no skin, but I still hold him tight. The sun is coming up now, and all's left is a pile of smoking wood—no Dad, no Mom, just me and Joey, and he is not crying. His blue eyes just stare. People come to help. They try to take Joey away from me, but I won't let him go. I say he will wake up real soon. It's morning now. Joey likes morning. The people are looking at me with sad faces. I say, 'Joey, you want pancakes?' But he just stares. 'Wake up Joey! Wake Up! Joey wake up!'

"I still see his beautiful li'l face smile and laugh at the breakfast table when we got pancakes for breakfast in the morning. Momma made the pancakes look like animals. I won't eat pancakes anymore because that was our brotherly thing to do. Maybe I will, if I get to heaven someday and hug my family again.

"Oh, well, kinda psychotherapy shit here, huh?"

Jan and Brianne shake their heads as they rub their eyes and cheeks with their cocktail napkins.

"I was in the hospital for almost a year for the burns. We didn't have any family that wanted to take me home. They said I was disfigured. They didn't want me. I was raised in an orphanage for disfigured, unwanted kids. It was a ranch, so we learned to work through or around our difficulties, as Roy and Edith ran the place and treated us like we were normal. I guess they knew the world would reject us, so they made us self-sufficient to live life as normal as possible. We did chores around the ranch. I learned to do cattle drives and respect the livestock. Roy and Edith were strict but always fair and would listen and help us.

"They loved us enough to toughen us up for the world that had choice words for us like gimp, freak, and others. Edith always said to me that if your so-called friends stop talking to you then it's because they're talking about you. She asked me, 'Do you know what you call those people, Luke? They are called gossips, and they're not friends to anybody. You just stay away from those folks Luke. They hiss like snakes. They are back stabbers.'

"That was good advice. See, us kids always got talked about because we are different. Not all of us have visible scars. Some of us brothers and sisters on the ranch have trouble learning, or talking well. We helped each other because nobody else cared for us. So yes, I love those kids and would love to have a job to give them joy, but also to prepare them for a cruel world and give them a skill that they would love to do. I'd like to be a Roy and Edith for those kids I see now at the stable." He inhales deeply.

"Ya know there was one thing that did survive the fire. It's this li'l Bible of my mom's." He reaches into his back pack. "It's kinda burned on the edges. I keep it in my back pack or saddle bags. It's the only thing left of my family. I guess I should read Mom's book, but I don't know how to read very well. People laugh at me for reading so slow, and that makes me feel dumb. But not the rodeo bull riding—nobody laughs at me there. They cheer, and I just keep my arms covered up.

"Mom's Bible has our family names." Luke turns the Bible so the others around the table can see her name, 'Betty Grieves, the wife of Bill and the mother of two sons, Luke and Joey, and baby Sarah will be born real soon.' How about that? I had a sister on the way. Maybe I will see her someday, do you think? I bet she would have loved mom's pancakes, too." Luke reclaims the Bible and hugs it to his chest.

"Oh, Luke, I am so sorry I gave you sass," Jan says.

"That's okay, Jan, I kinda ack like an ass to hide this shit here. I don't want people to think I am weak. I don't cry ever. Sorry I broke tonight. I lost everything I knew in one day. You just never know do ya?"

"Don't ever apologize for a few tears," Richard grimaces. That's a whole lot better than booze. I speak from experience."

"I missed out on all my Momma's hugs, ya know. I don't really know how families act."

Richard snorts, "I don't think any of us knows how a real family acts. Most of them I've seen are pretty dysfunctional. But if you can find a way to follow your calling to work with kids, I think that's what you should do."

"Luke," Jan sniffles, "Brianne and I may get a little money someday, and maybe we can start a charity for orphans for you to run."

Richard adds, "Luke, I am sorry for my watery eyes too. I never knew your past was so tragic. I see so much evil in my work, that I lose the human part of it. I see what people do, but I don't think about what happened in their lives to cause it. Maybe you have taught me to be more compassionate from now on."

"Yeah, Richard, I hope so. You slammed me pretty hard. It was like a bull throwing me into a fence."

"I am sorry about that. I need to do something about my temper. I didn't have a bad one when Crystal was alive.

"My wife, Crystal, ran a lot of charities, and she was well connected. I will call her friends when I get back from our trip, and we will start a Crystal, Joey and Sarah Charity Fund for disabled children, whether orphaned or not, and we will get ponies, goats, donkeys—whatever you want Luke."

Luke wipes tears from his eyes and looks down, shaking his head in disbelief. Jan stands, takes the few steps necessary to reach him, and plops onto his lap. She cups his face with her small hands lifting his chin up, and gives him a big, long kiss right on his mouth, and she hugs him real tight.

That brought a smile through Luke's tears! "Thank you, Jan, but I don't understand what you see in me now that I broke down in front of you, and I look like a weak man crying like a baby."

"Luke, showing me your vulnerabilities makes you the strongest and most handsome man I have ever known. Your arm burns show your courage, and the love you have for your brother Joey should be envied and copied. You had a man's trial as a boy and became a man at five years old. Any woman would be lucky to be hugged by these scarred arms that have proven by fire the love you hold in your heart. Scars of love? I would like to have them around me, Luke."

Richard remarks, "Luke, you have had your problems on

the job, but I can kind of understand now why. For your new endeavor, you will need an office to get it all going, and it can't be the bunkhouse. So I would like to offer you my guest house to start the operation. You need a suit and nicer clothes to work with the affluent town folks and when you ask for donations. I will have someone help you write your story. That is a powerful one that will open the wallets of the wealthy I know.

"I will be leaving tomorrow, so let me show you around my place now. I know your driving record is good, and I don't want that oil dripping peace of shit El Camino of yours on my driveway, so you can use my truck to get around. To start, we will go to the station to let the men know what's up and who it is staying at my place.

"Jerri is shopping for sailing attire, getting ready for the trip, and she also bought a flashlight that she took the batteries out of and filled with Agape sand just in case she needs it to catch Clark. She is also taking extra pairs of the Agape glasses."

"Jerri's really going with you?" Jan shrieks. "How did you convince her to do that?"

"I'm the detective on the case, and she wants it solved as badly as I do."

Jan shakes her head unbelievingly and disapprovingly.

* * * * *

The morning comes. Jerri and Richard meet Bill at the dock in Long Beach at the beautiful sailing vessel *Nui Koa* and make introductions. Bill invites them aboard where he introduces his young daughter of fourteen, Anakalia, who is part of the crew. She also is a trained captain.

Bill instructs the newcomers on wearing the life vests and what are the safe areas on the vessel to keep from getting hit by the boom. He has given each one a job to do because this is a race, and everyone works on this vessel, but what a once in a life time experience!

"Hey, Jerri, I have kind of a jittery stomach with excitement," Richard whispers to her as the vessel glides smoothly away from the dock.

"Me, too, Richard, but I think the race is the easy part of this journey. Clark is a different story. He is demon possessed. I would never believe it, but I saw it."

Now outside the breakwater, Bill gives instructions to his crew, and they teach Jerri and Richard what is required of them. The wind has picked up and the crew runs up the spinnaker. It fills with air, ballooning out as the vessel picks up speed quickly. Richard and Jerri are making way to Diamond Head.

Chapter 10
Revival

Back in Ocean Crest, there seems to be a revival at the Ocean Crest Community Church. The small fellowship of maybe fifty or so that includes Crystal's parents, are starting to see an increase of curious younger folks looking for answers. They walk in with wide-eyed urgency and fear—not of the Church, but they want answers because of the haunting of their dreams at night from the shadow-man demon.

The marquee out in front of the church this week reads,

The cure for nightmares

1 John 4: 1-4: "*[1]Dear friends, do not believe every spirit, but test the spirits to see whether they are from God, because many false prophets have gone out into the world.*"

The theme continues on the bulletin with, "*[2]This is how you can recognize the Spirit of God: Every spirit that acknowledges that Jesus Christ has come in the flesh is from God, [3]but every spirit that does not acknowledge Jesus is not from God. This is the spirit of the antichrist, which you have heard is coming and even now is already in the world.*

"*[4]You, dear children, are from God and have overcome them, because the one who is in you is greater than the one who is in the world.*"

These young visitors have heard that the church-goers in the town are not visited at night by the demon. Well, that is true, because the believers have the Holy Spirit living in them and are protected by God as His children.

However, going to church doesn't save anyone. Many people go and hear the Word but miss the "narrow gate."

Matthew 7:13-14; "*Enter through the narrow gate. For wide is the gate and broad is the road that leads to destruction, and many enter through it. But small is the gate and narrow the road that leads to life, and only a few find it.*"

Then, sort of as a PS, the bulletin added John 10:7, "Then Jesus said to them..., 'I am the door…"

The heaviness of the oppressive spirit is now felt even by strangers when entering the Ocean Crest city limits.

Even the animals act jumpy as that evil cloud moves around and through the city until it passes once more.

Only to return.

Chapter 11
Battle Your Demons

Jack Clark, DVM, sails onward into the rolling blue seas tormented by many ghosts in his head saying, *"Jack, you failed. You missed the kill. You swallowed the Voodoo brew like the other three, but you failed us Jack!"*

Clark holds the ship's wheel tightly and shakes his head violently, as if he is trying to shake demons from his mind. He screams to the sky, "You beasts! You made me kill my wife. Ahhhhhhhhhhhh, I am a madman! Now I'm on the run taking you beasts to the island of the tree demons. So stop your torment in my head! Get the hell out of me!"

"Jack you drank the swill and invited us in to make the kill, with a home in your head. That is your will. We are your life now, and we will be your death. You are just a taxi ride 'til you take your last breath. We can't be cast out of you because you hated Carolann's God and his only Son. So shut your damn mouth, or we will make you screaming mad. Your mind will be undone!"

Clark lapsed into quiet thought, *I hate that smartass bitch Jerri. She took my eye. I want her to be dead! I will add her to the three others, Carolann, Crystal, and that first cowgirl bitch that bit my hand behind the Mule kick saloon. I took a drink of that Voodoo brew, and now that bitch's life is permanently through. So, she didn't like that I grabbed her big bust; ashes to ashes and dust to dust; crematory fire burns much hotter than a midnight's lust; she has disappeared forever in a desert wind gust.*

Clark sails on through the sea, wrestling and arguing with his demons as he trims the sails. His appearance is now of a mad man—unshaven face twitches, outbursts of cursing, burning fire in his eye. This man is gone—forever possessed he will die.

Satan's Marionette

James Ruether

Tempted by the fiery strings you embrace the devils dance

Lust of power, fame and riches your drawn into the trance

Satan's fiery strings snare the materialistic marionette

The stage spotlights your dancing shadow but casts Satan's

Silhouette

Whirlpool of emotion:
Drowning in worthlessness. The spinning vortex surrounds;
ghosted text—Rejection.
I'm not worth your reply. To Hopelessness I'm bound.
Swirling under scarlet liquid. Descending into darkness.
Treading arms weaken so I sink—Down.
Desperate for gasps of air.
My dizzying life of loneliness Murmurs in my ear.
You're a Living disappointment. To all this I must admit.
To the lonely depths I must now submit.
Demons claw at my heels To pull me from the light.
My Life? I now lose my grip.
Tired of this struggle. I am all out of fight./
I now fall into the abyss, Terminating my light.

Chapter 12
Luke's New Life Chapter

Luke and Jan meet at the bunkhouse for the big move into Richard's guest house. Kicking the door open to #2, they walk across the worn, dusty, wood floor of the room that has one small bed, a hat rack, a small kitchen, a bathroom with shower—a very plain and simple room fitting for a dusty cowboy bull rider.

They sit next to each other on the bed. Luke clasps his hands between his knees and stares at them as he says, "Jan, I have to admit something. I'm scared that I may fail at this opportunity because I can't read well, and this looks like a lot of book work. And it will hurt me to fail these kids like I did Joey."

Jan takes his hands in one of hers and uses the other one to tilt his head toward her. "Luke!" she says tenderly but decisively, "you did not fail your brother. You tried to save him, and that may not have been possible because, the way you described the story, and me working with pets that have been in a fire sometimes, the fire goes into the lungs damaging them so badly they cannot any longer support life. Luke, your brother faced a fireball when he was screaming, and that is what killed him. Nobody could have saved him after that."

"Thank you, Jan. You're so smart." He looked at her earnestly. "Jan, I want to see my family again. My momma always said to me that we will all be together in Heaven someday. She always drew me a map of how to get places, like the bus stop. Do you think she left this Bible book for me to find in the ashes as a map to her?"

"That is not a bad way to look at it," Jan frowns as she puzzles, "because why didn't it burn?"

"Jan, I can't read the word map in this book, but maybe I could take it to an expert to ask how to get to Mom. Maybe that church knows how to read this word map. Would you go with me to ask that preacher guy?"

"Okay," Jan stammers, "I guess that would be fun."

"Fun? What do you mean fun? What's fun about that Jan?"

"I have a pair of the Agape glasses to see what's going on with the hypocrites in the church," Jan giggles.

"I don't know what you're talking about, but okay," Luke shrugs.

Jan pats Luke's leg as she stands up and says, "All right! Let's get moving!"

They load up Luke's stuff, including an old taped together suitcase and a duffle bag, and make the move to Richard's guest house.

Jan drives Luke to the guest house because he can't bring his oil-dripping, piece of shit pickup there, and they enter the house. Grace greets them with a smile.

"Would you kids like some tacos to snack on while you unpack?" Grace asks.

"Well," drawls Luke, "I'm no kid, but your offer sounds pretty good, Ma'am. My name is Luke and you are?"

"Grace. My name is Grace, and the boss gave me instructions to help you settle in."

"Well, thank you, Grace. I don't want to put you out any, Ma'am."

"I'm Grace, not Ma'am," she says as she plunks a few tacos on the table for the pair. Mr. Luke, go ahead and give me your belongings because I am supposed to wash them first thing." Grace takes the clothes from Luke and says, "Luke, Richard wants you to visit his tailor today for measurements for some stylish attire all paid for. The truck keys are on the table." She leaves for the laundry room.

Luke almost chokes on his taco. "Wow! Things are moving fast! Jan, if you're not too busy, would you help me today and tomorrow... and other days too?"

"Yes, I will help you get started. I hope to be a part of this charity in a big way."

"I want you to do that, too. I am nervous, but not when you are with me."

"Luke, I like this side of you. You're not the smartass that you were at the stables."

"This is who I always have been, but I can't let people know me because then they see me as weak. And, boy, that's not a good rep for a bull rider. People are cruel, and they use you and they heartlessly toss your heart in the trash when you no longer meet their needs."

"Are you talking about an old girlfriend, Luke? It sounds like it to me, and that's okay. You can talk to me. I am a safe person for you to confide in."

"Yeah, we were together for about two years, and one day she just said, 'Let's just be friends now.' It all was fine, like she really loved me up to that day—all smiles and kisses, but then she just flipped to hating me—just like that!" Luke snaps his fingers. "I still don't know why even now. She didn't answer her phone no more. It was just like I was dead. I cried for months when I was alone. It hurts so bad, even now, because her not telling me why. That makes me think I have no value as a person, and I should be dead. Silence is the most cruel thing someone can do to another person. I would bet that a weaker man may have taken his own life. I guess she didn't like the fact that I was different."

Jan reached over and took Luke's hands in hers. "It's her loss Luke, you are the best man any woman could want. She used you and left you because she lacked any character of her own and had nothing to offer you anyway. And maybe her silence was better than any words she had to say. So... good riddance to her. She is just empty, heartless, and just trouble. She will do the same to many more poor unsuspecting guys, so, Luke, look at me, okay? It's not you! She is a Delilah."

"How did you know her name? I didn't say it." Luke pulls away from her hold and looked at her suspiciously.

Jan laughs as she drops his hands. "My mom always told us girls not to be like Delilah, who was the bad woman who brought down Samson. She was an amorous, delightful, languishing temptress who seduced men for gain to fill her emptiness. That's what my mom always said. I don't know about her, but your girlfriend sounds just like this, Luke."

"You're right, Jan, she fits her name."

Grace comes in with some more tacos and says, "Did you guys know that there are news reporters in the town interviewing people about the hauntings?"

"What? Ocean Crest is popular for ghosts now? Oh, boy!" Jan sighs. "Ya' know, after Brianne found out about Clark trying to kill my sister, she told me that one night she couldn't sleep so she went to the stables and saddled up Bentley for a moonlight ride. She galloped down to the surf, and they ran through the spray in the moonlight. On their way back to the stables, she felt a chill crawl up her back. She looked behind her and saw a shadowy man on a horse rushing at her with a polo mallet swinging over his head. She kicked Bentley, and he took off running hard. They outran the guy, but she was pretty shook up at the stables. So she strapped on her Colt .45 from her truck while she put Bentley away.

"This, she said, was a month ago. Then she thought to herself that maybe it was in her imagination, so she didn't mention it. Besides, who would have believed a story like that? I mean, Sleepy Hollow with the headless horseman—it sounds so similar. It's always funny that, in hindsight, strange and unbelievable stories may turn out to be real."

* * * * *

Favorable winds of the Pacific pull at the billowing sails reaching out to Hawaii. Onward the sleek graceful hull of the *Great Warrior* slices the swaying seas.

* * * * *

Luke settles in at Richard's house with his new wardrobe

of business suits that he is definitely not comfortable in. Sunday has come around, so Jan picks Luke up to head for church.

"Hey, Luke, you're wearing your cowboy duds today to church," Jan says.

"Yeah, I am just me, and I got my Book."

Jan and Luke pull into the church parking lot in Jan's hot little rumbling truck that does turn some heads. They walk up to the doors, and the pastor smiles and greets them warmly.

"Most of the folks here say good morning and welcome us in, and during the introductions nobody looks down on how we are dressed." Jan whispers to Luke.

Luke says, "Just wait. See that older lady with the flowered hat back there talking to the one in the yellow dress? Well, I saw her point at us out of the side of my eye and whisper shit. What are you doing, Jan?"

"I'm putting on my glasses. Wow, Luke, I will tell you when we leave, but most everyone in here has a pure heart except those two gossips. They are slightly angry. I don't know why our hearts aren't like the pure ones. Maybe I can find out here."

Nothing too crazy here, Jan thought, *just sing a few songs and Pastor reads the Book and says how it is a letter from God to us.*

The service is over, and the Pastor comes up to Luke, shakes his hand and says, "Luke, I have been expecting you."

"What do you mean, expecting me?"

"God put it on my heart this week that a cowboy would visit with questions about His Word."

"You mean this Book?" Luke held his Bible out toward the pastor.

"Yes."

"This Bible book my Mom had went through a fire, but it is still readable. Can you tell me what map in here will help me to find my mom? My mom always made me maps before she died."

"Well, yes, Luke, she gave you a map to Heaven. That's

where she is, but it is a person that can show you the way to her. You have to meet this person and accept him as family."

"Show me that person who knows where Heaven is, Please, Pastor, I gotta find her."

"Luke, the person is the Son of God, Jesus. Your momma knew Him through reading this Book. Luke did your family pray or say grace at your dinner table before you ate your food?"

"Yeah, Dad said a prayer at supper time."

"Luke, they were talking to God. If you seek Him, you will find Him. He said that to all the world."

"I don't read well. I can't find Him in the Book."

"That's okay. Many people can't read, and they are saved, Luke. He asks us to believe in Him and believe that He came into the world to save us from our sins and take our place on the cross. He said believe and trust like children for 'of such is the Kingdom of Heaven'."

"Am I childish? Luke asks Jan."

Jan looks Luke in the eyes and says, "No, Luke, you are not childish; you are childlike, innocent. You have a young heart."

"Okay," Luke addresses the pastor, "I will come back again if you don't mind me asking a lot of questions."

"You are always welcome here, Luke, and you are, too, Ma'am."

"I'm Jan, Pastor."

"I'm happy to meet you both. Thank you for coming today. I look forward to seeing you often. Do you have any questions right now?"

"Yes," Luke stammered, "you said we had to believe and trust like children. How do we do that?"

"Children trust adults and believe immediately what they are told by them. We need to do that with God's Word. Luke, Jan, I gave a message about entering through the narrow gate. Jesus is the narrow gate to God's Kingdom. When we put our

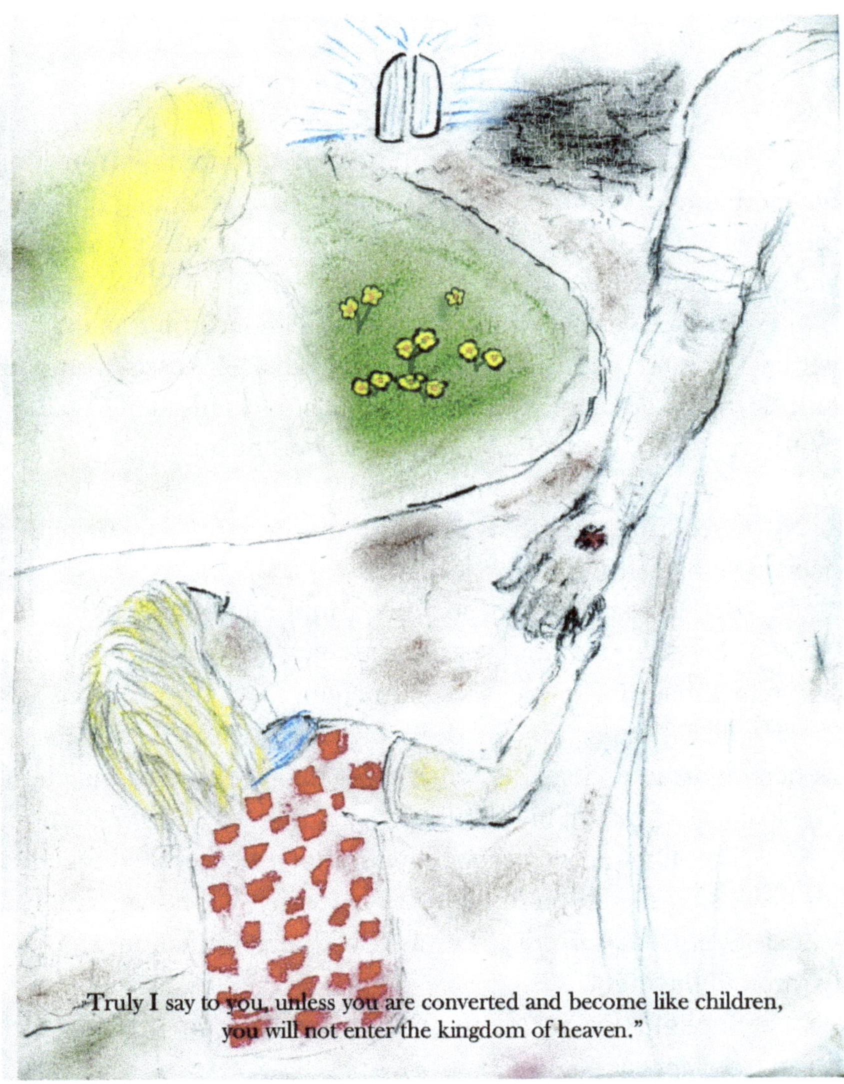

hand in His and follow Him through life, we become part of His kingdom.

"God made salvation simple and a free gift to save people from destruction."

As the pastor speaks, Jan visualizes herself becoming as a child and reaching for the scarred hand of Jesus.

Chapter 13

Island of the Tree Demons

Nui Koa finishes at the top of the race and now is making way to Palmyra Atoll. Tension fills the boat, and talking quiets as the yacht closes in on the island. It is the night watch at the helm, and Bill has entrusted Richard to take the wheel.

The heavens sparkle like bright diamonds on a black velvet background, and waves gently slap the sleek vessel's smooth hull. Jerri sits down next to Richard and studies his star-lit face—a little rugged now that he has grown a short beard.

"What are you looking at, Jerri?"

"Security and strength inside the heart of a man with a handsome and strong face."

Richard smiles and puts his arm around her, pulling her close to his side, making her feel safe and loved. Someday they will remember this journey as sentimental.

"It will be over soon, Jerri," Richard whispers, as he kisses her forehead and squeezes her tight into the side of his chest. She leans her head on his shoulder.

The night ocean breeze caresses their peaceful silhouettes, for now, as they sail on to their life's destiny, unknown, The Hawaiian *Great Warrior* vessel cruises with determination, smoothly through the night.

Sunlight kisses them good morning as in the distance green trees appear.

Jerri goes down inside to wake the captain for Richard.

Bill comes topside. "What's up, Richard?"

"Look, Bill, I see the island, and I don't know how shallow the reefs are here or where to steer to come into the island."

"Okay, Richard, good job. It will be a couple hours before we arrive, so you go get some sleep. My daughter and I can handle it from here."

"Thanks, Bill."

Bill skillfully steers the vessel through the shallows as they approach the island. No other boats are in sight as he anchors on the protected side of the island.

They have made good time and may be a day or more ahead of Clark. After many days at sea, they eagerly blow up a raft and paddle to shore to stand on stable ground. The beauty of this island is beyond description; however there is the feeling of being watched from the trees. Creepy feelings crawl up their backs, but they can't see anything. There is a feeling that they are trespassing and not wanted here.

Jerri decides to put on her Agape glasses and look around the island.

"Richard!" Jerri calls, "I can't make them out, but in the trees, I see spots of black whirlwind clouds just like I saw over the hearts of evil people, but there are no visible bodies like the people. Take a look."

"I left my glasses on the boat." She hands him one of the extra pairs glasses she's made as he strides up beside her.

"You're right, Jerri, and the black clouds fly from tree to tree. You can't see them without the glasses on—whatever they are."

Bill wanders along side them and explains, "There have been many shipwrecks here and pirates' stolen treasure stories, and brutal murders. There are believed to be many ghosts on this island, so let's make this visit very brief." Just then a coconut sails right by his head.

"What the...? See? I'm not sleeping on this Island tonight! We'd better stay on the boat. Something wants us gone—probably the pirates' ghosts."

They paddle back out to the *Warrior* and string out some fishing lines to catch a fresh dinner. Jerri starts singing some songs, and Bill brings up his ukulele and joins in singing "Somewhere Over the Rainbow". They spend a delightful afternoon catching fish and making a wonderful dinner. It's been a marathon trip, and they enjoy each others' company just relaxing.

They are anchored out about two hundred yards off the island. Night falls, and the stars shine brightly, Jerri puts her glasses on. Looking at the island, she sees the black clouds with red in them going from tree to tree.

It's a quiet night, so they turn in to their bunks.

The sun breaks through the night and rises up over the ocean. Jerri is the first one up, and she makes coffee in the galley before she goes up on deck. The coffee aroma is beckoning the others to awaken.

Jerri pours a cup and finally steps up on deck. She surveys the ocean scape and sees a boat anchored a hundred yards away—the sailboat with *Holo Aku* on the stern. Jerri runs below.

"Richard, Bill, there's a boat with the name *Holo Aku* on the back!"

Bill spurts, "That's the name, Richard! That name means *Sail Away*. That's Clark, guys!"

Richard says, "It's time for a plan. He may not recognize me with this beard, so maybe surprise is the best bet in catching him."

"Richard," Jerri objects, "he has the strength of ten men, so how can you overpower that?"

Bill interrupts, "What's that noise? It sounds like an eerie chorus of loud wailings?"

"Look on the beach," Jerri whispers, "Clark is shouting at the trees with a hundred voices coming out of his mouth, and the trees are shouting back. It's like demons are greeting each other."

Then Clark snaps his wild head in their direction and stares.

Richard recovers quickly. "The three of us will go back to shore now, and I will arrest Jack."

"My daughter will stay and watch the vessel," Bill says.

Jerri looks faint.

"Jerri, can you do this?"

"I think so, but I haven't seen his face since he tried to kill me. What's stopping him this time?"

"I will stop him! He will be in cuffs in a few minutes. Jerri." *Is Richard overconfident?* Jerri wonders.

"Where's your gun, Richard?" Jerri asks.

"I didn't bring it because I may just kill him. So I will get him with my bare hands." Jerri shrugs dubiously.

"Richard," Bill interrupted, "I am bringing my shark tooth ax to shore, just in case."

"Okay, but I don't think he will be a problem. I could always beat him in wrestling in school."

As they paddle to shore to confront Jack, Jerri hands each man a pair of Agape glasses and gives Bill a quick explanation..

They disembark, Bill speaks, "Hi, I am Bill, and these happy honeymooners are John and Linda."

"Why are you all here?" Jack's voice roars. "You're not welcome on our island!"

Jack hasn't recognized Richard and Jerri yet. She had dyed her hair blonde, and Richard's beard is quite full.

"What's your name, Sir?" Bill inquires.

"You won't be here long enough to exchange pleasantries, so leave now!" Clark shouts back.

Richard walks up to Jack and extends his arm as if to shake his hand. Jack jumps back as Richard lunges and grabs Jack's arm to pull it up behind his back as they fall to the ground.

"You're under arrest for the murder of Crystal Michaels," Richard yells as he holds him on the ground to cuff him like he has done to others a thousand times before.

Jerri put on her glasses and sees the trees moving violently without a breeze. The demons become visible through the glasses as Jack's face turns bright red.

Suddenly, from his lying position with Richard on top of him, Jack springs up ten feet in the air screaming, "I should have killed you, Bitch. Now I know who you are, and you are all going to die!" He flings Richard.

Richard flies backward through the air hitting a tree knocking him dizzy. Jack glances at Richard, "I will deal with you after I kill your bitch. Come here, Bitch, I will make it quick."

Jack stalks up to Jerri as she leans back, frozen with fear, against the trunk of a tree. Jack reaches for her delicate neck to crush it, and from her locket fire shoots out, setting Jack's arm ablaze.

He screams in pain and backs off. Bill makes a running tackle knocking Jack down to the ground again. Richard regains his balance and jumps on Jack's back. This time, he and Bill together cuff Jack's hands behind his back.

"Wow! I got you now," Richard yells at Jack.

Jack rolls over and sits up. With an evil smile he snarls, "You don't have shit. We will never be subdued by you mortals. You will be our next meal!"

The trees sway, roaring with demon voices. Through her Agape glasses, Jerri can see smoky forms. She stands stunned, remembering Jack's incredible power when he attacked her. She sneaks a look at the battle.

Jack Clark smiles at Richard, "This is going to be fun. Now you will join Crystal, your ugly bitch wife. All her Christian shit couldn't save her, so I took her life. She said that she forgave me. That was her last breath, her soft eyes stared up at me as I strangled her to death."

Richard charges at Jack screaming, "I will kill you, you bastard! You are dead!"

Richard hits Jack like a football tackle, and as they fall Jack breaks the handcuffs more easily than spreading butter. Laughing, he stands up and throws Richard 20 feet away. Then he walks over to his dirty sports bag. He opens it, and stacks of money pour out. From the bottom, he lifts up a glass jar.

"Hey, Richard, I am not here alone see? I brought my wife, Carolanne, her ashes are all in this clear jar. She was too much like Crystal, so I smashed her head too. You'll tell no one because now we will kill you!"

Jack reaches down in his bag and pulls out a polo mallet. He walks to Richard, who still lies dazed from being tossed so far. Jack raises the mallet up over his head.

Bill throws his shark tooth ax, hitting Jacks neck and severing a major artery. Blood gushes out from the mortal wound.

Dropping the mallet, Jack staggers. Holding his neck, he glares at Bill. "You're next to die, Captain!"

Jack's neck wound heals completely in a moment as his evil smile returns. "I am invincible with my friends inside me," Jack laughs. He turns and jumps on Richard and grabs his neck in a stranglehold.

"You're dead now, old friend. You'll never look down on me again."

Richard grasps Jack's hands, trying to break his grip, as Jack snarls down at him.

Jerri screams Richard's name as she runs to the struggling pair and jumps on Jack. She sticks her finger in Jack's good eye socket. He throws her off him as if she were an insect.

He lets go of Richard to chase Jerri. He tackles her to the ground. Fire from her necklace sets his whole body aflame. Screeching, he jumps off Jerri to run back to kill Richard. Filled with demons, he has superhuman strength, but his mind seems to be frenzied.

"Get out of here Jerri! Go back to the ship! You and Anakalia sail away to safety!" Bill commands Jerri. She shakes her head.

They are all in a moment going to meet their death. Jack had said then they would eat their flesh.

Clark grabs Richard and lifts him above his head like a trophy before he would smash him on the ground.

Jerri's mind flashes onto an idea from her fire shooting charm. She grabs her flashlight and opens it for the Agape sand. It becomes energized as she throws the sand on Jack Clark.

"Let Richard go!" Jerri screams.

Clark looks at Jerri and drops Richard as he bursts into flame—standing with his arms out away from his sides. He is burning but is not consumed. He leans his head back with his mouth open wide. The screaming demons, on fire, shoot out of his mouth. Departing their host, the hundreds of burning demons clog the air—flying, circling around in the sky, eclipsing the sun. The tree demons join them in the air, creating darkness. As the last demon leaves Jack, he falls weakly on his face.

"Wow!" Bill shouts as the three stand there looking dazed. "I'm sure glad we had these glasses, or we wouldn't have seen the whole story!"

Richard strides purposefully toward Jack saying, "I will cuff him now that he has lost his power."

The sight of the whirling dark demons in the sky strikes fear in them all. The burning demons circle in the air screaming, "Death to you all!"

Where the Agape sand hit the ground, the island sand starts to rumble and shake. The sand in a circle twenty feet wide starts spinning, and everyone jumps back as the center falls into a chasm. Flames shoot up out of the hole.

They hear screams and moans coming up from the depths, and then lizard-like claws clutch at the edge, trying to climb out of the pit. A deafening, roaring wind sound comes up from the depths. A tornado of flame shoots up to the sky grabbing the demons from their flight and pulling them into the vortex of flame, sucking the ancient tree demons along with the rest. The instant they are sucked into the pit, the pit seals closed like it never was there. The island is at rest now. The evil is gone.

Weak and cuffed, Jack sobs, "You guys, I am so sorry for all I did. I was hooked on that potion in that jar next to the bag.

When I drank it, I would be overcome with evil and could not stop myself. Where did it go? Was it was sucked into the hole?"

They all look around, and not seeing the potion jar, they assume it was consumed by the sand pit.

"I will go back willingly. I will not trouble you anymore, Richard, or you either, Jerri," Jack sobs. "And I guess you should know I sent that text to Fabian sending him to your place for a phony catering interview.

"Richard, can we put Carolann's ashes in my money bag and bring them all home?" Jack asked.

"Yes, Jack, they are evidence anyway."

They paddle out to the *Warrior* and board the vessel. For a few moments, they all collapse on the deck. "Whew!" mutters Bill, "that was one wild ride he took us on."

"For sure," agrees Richard, "but the three of us were not winning. We could not have come out alive without Jerri's Agape sand." The others nod.

"Richard, I don't want to ride back with him on the boat," Jerri shudders. "I can't look at him. Maybe you could send someone for me? I will stay here on the island."

"You don't want to do that, Jerri," Bill says. "It's okay to take a boat home. I am going to have Anakalia captain his vessel back to the mainland, so you can sail with her—just you two girls."

"That's a great idea, Bill. The vessel will be impounded, and I will deputize all of you guys right now," Richard explains. "Jerri, if it were not for you and your sand, we would all be dead now. I don't know what I just witnessed, but it has to be supernatural."

"I don't know either, Richard, but maybe we will figure it out when we get home," Jerri responds.

"Okay, Sweetie," Bill instructs his daughter, "go check out your new vessel and make sure it squares away with all the provisions you will need for a month."

Jerri looks at Richard and sighs. "This slow sail back home will give me some time to collect my thoughts and relax a bit."

"You deserve it, Jerri. You have had a rough four and a half years, but now maybe your nightmares will be gone for good."

Bill maps out a course for Anakalia and Jerri to follow. The weather looks good. Both vessels have the best GPS and electronics available on board.

Jerri transfers her belongings over to the *Holo Aku.* Upon entering the cabin, she sees this is a luxury vessel with shower, kitchen, double beds, and is fully stocked with food—very classy.

This is perfect no more nightmares just peace at sea.

On Bill's vessel, Richard gets down to business. "Okay. let's get out of here and get Jack back to the mainland.

"Jack; You have the right to remain silent. If you do say anything, what you say can be used against you in a court of law. You have the right to consult with a lawyer and have that lawyer present during any questioning. If you cannot afford a lawyer, one will be appointed for you if you so desire. If you choose to talk to the police officer, you have the right to stop the interview at any time.

"Do you understand these rights?"

"Yes, Richard. I am not talking," Jack states.

The vessels lift up anchors and steer the course home.

"I want to ask one thing of Bill, Richard."

"Okay, he is the captain," Richard shrugs.

"What's your question, Jack?" Bill snaps.

"What the hell was that thing you threw at me cutting my neck?"

"That's a Great Hawaiian Warriors' shark tooth ax. You would have been dead if not for that evil power. That was a mortal wound I delivered to you."

"You are a master at your throwing accuracy."

"That's right! I am a Great Hawaiian Warrior, Jack! Now you keep your mouth shut on my vessel *Nui Koa,* The Great Warrior, not another word from you!"

"Boy, my friend," Richard claps Bill on his shoulder. "I didn't know I signed you up for this. You are a hero, Bill, to risk your life so save us."

"Richard, we can all share that title. We all faced death and didn't run," Bill replied.

"Actually, it was Jerri's quick thinking with throwing the Agape sand on him that saved us, Bill."

"You're right, Richard. She's a smart girl. I think she a keeper," Bill smiles.

"I think you're right, Bill," Richard mumbles. "I think you're right."

* * * * *

Nui Koa sails out ahead of the *Holo Aku* making their way back to the States. This trip promises to be long and peaceful for the women, with just the wind and the sea for company. Jerri spends many starlit nights reflecting on her past and pondering her future as she holds her locket tight.

Oh, God, so many stars You cast from Your hand to sparkle the night. I hold Your loving power in my locket under the stars so bright. I feel Your love in my hand, but You are out of my sight. How do I put Your locket-love in my heart before the sun removes the night?

God, You have saved my life with this sand now three or four times, and I feel safe—as if You are with me after this traumatic fight on the beach. I feel safe with You and secure and loved with Richard. He has what the other men lacked. If we have a future, Lord, have Richard greet me at the dock by saying "welcome ashore, Your Highness." Then I will know.

Chapter 14
Crystals Closure

The city of Ocean Crest has returned to what it was before the murders, and the night hauntings suddenly cease. The animals are calm now. The town doesn't know why, but the five who witnessed the demons disappear from the sky know.

Richard booked Jack Clark into the Ocean Crest City Jail a week ago, and now it's time to complete Crystal's request and finally put her to rest.

Richard walks into the kitchen and pours his morning coffee that Grace has prepared. Then he walks slowly through his home from room to room gazing at the paintings throughout their home that Crystal had painted, as well as photographs, and the mementos that were dear to her. The beautiful portrait of her sitting in her favorite spot in the garden on the prayer bench, dressed in her flowered blue dress with her beautiful face's bright smile and her hands crossed on her lap is displayed in the most honorable place at the center of the home over the fireplace mantle. Richard looks at her portrait as he hugs the leather saddle bags that contain her ashes. A tear drop from his eye makes a spot on the leather bag but does not break his focus from her. *I can now put you to rest, my sweetheart. I know it's been so long. I will hold you tight in my arms for awhile this one last time before I set you forever free.*

I don't understand why your God took you from me. I never have known such a love—that you could forgive a man as he was destroying you. Is this the love that is called Agape? I believe you must be right about Jesus, because now I know, and I have seen that there really is a hell. I think God brought Jerri into my life with His power because there was no other way to stop Jack without the Agape sand. I miss you so much. I miss you signing to me in the morning.

He wanders through the French doors and into the garden.

I miss seeing you on your bench reading and the way you would close your book and look up at me smiling when I entered the garden. You patted the bench seat so I would sit close to you. I put my arm around you, and we would sit, sharing a happy moment in time—enjoying it together, not saying a single word. The birds sang, the rabbits hopped, and the tree squirrels chattered above. Your bright red roses that you planted here and there— red is the color that you love. Honey bees abuzz doing their labor of love throughout this garden of beauty. This garden spot is a sacred place, Crystal. You made it so.

You calmed the rage in my heart that no other woman could do, but it returned after we were apart. Five years I have shown a temper, but now it has become calm again since Jerri came into my life. Richard turns slowly to gaze at the entire garden. *She is not like you, but in so many good ways she is. Her heart is generous, loving and kind. This kind of woman nowadays is impossible to find. But there is a piece of her heart broken that maybe only your God can fix. Anyway, Sweet Crystal, Jerri should be arriving home in a week or so. Then you can ride Bentley for the last time to the sea. Your ashes will be gone, but your memory will always be with me.*

Many more spots appear on the leather bag, tears now falling down from his sad eyes almost like rain. Richard returns to the house and looks again upon her portrait. Reaching up with his trembling fingers to the canvas they stretch out lovingly to touch her face again. He drops his head and turns away, walking out of the room. Reality hits Richard really hard again. He needs to walk away.

* * * * *

Brianne is busy at the stables making contacts to buy animals that are gentle for the disabled children to experience. She has a miniature horse named Mini Cooper and is inquiring around for some baby goats, ponies. and donkeys. She had ordered hay for the new horses and goats. The flat bed truck pulls into the stables loaded with hay. The sign on the truck door reads Jesús & Son Trucking, and there is a little head sticking up on the passenger side with a bigger-than-life smile.

Jan says, "That is Jerri's little friend." The truck stops, and Jan walks up to the passenger door. "Hi, Jesús, you may not know me, but I am Dr. Jerri's sister, Jan."

"Is my Dr. Jerri here? I miss her. Does she remember me?"

"Oh, yes, Jesús, she loves you and tells everyone how proud she is of you. Did you hurt your eye I see you have a patch?"

"I am a pirate. I have a sword here too, see? Where is Doctor Jerri?"

"She is on a sailboat in the ocean on her way home now."

"I should be with her to protect her with my sword. Can I go on her ship?"

"Can I go pet that li'l horse over there?" the vibrant child asks Brianne.

Jan was relieved when Jesús's attention was diverted. "Why yes, Jesús. His name is Mini Cooper, and he loves to be petted."

The polo club is investing in a special area with a petting zoo and corral. They are also furnishing safety helmets and special saddles to strap the children on the horses.

Word spreads about the charity for Crystal, Joey and Sarah, and the town responds generously. Crystal is still much beloved in this town, and this is a perfect cause to donate to. Many people have volunteered to serve with the kids and help with all the red tape, lawyers, and accountants, and the whole equestrian community wants to serve or be on the board.

Luke's greatest fear has been lifted off his shoulders with

so much professional help on the paper work, which is not his strong area of expertise, being offered.

* * * * *

The day has arrived. Jerri and young Captain Anakalia Boyd sail safely into the harbor. Richard meets them at the dock and ties the ropes. He reaches his hand out to Jerri and helps her ashore.

"Welcome ashore, Your Highness!" Richard grins, pauses, and sobers. "I missed you, Jerri. You look so great—rested and tan and wearing your bright smile."

"I was thinking of you, too, Richard; collecting my thoughts and thinking of my plans for the future."

"Do you see me in your future, Jerri?"

Jerri smiles, just looking up at Richard for a moment that seems to last forever. She doesn't say a word. She reaches up with her hands and pulls his face down for a long, passionate kiss.

Jerri smilingly asks, "Does this answer your question, Sir?"

Richard smiles and hugs her tight. "Yes, Ma'am. I was hoping that you felt the same as I do. Come on! Let's get you home. I want to celebrate your safe return." They walk hand in hand to the car.

"Jerri, you said you were thinking about our future while you were sailing home. What are your thoughts?"

Gazing at the ground, Jerri answered slowly. "Richard, I missed you, but I haven't had any success picking men. So I asked God for a sign that we would be a match." She stops walking and talking.

When she didn't continue, Richard asks, "Did you get the sign yet, Jerri?"

She giggles and gazes at him with sparkling eyes. "Yes, it was for you to say 'Welcome ashore, Your Highness'. That's why it took me a minute to respond. I couldn't believe the surprise."

"This makes me so happy!" Richard pulls her close for a

hug. "I was worried about you with all the trauma you experienced, and I couldn't be there to help you." They start strolling again. "Jerri, I had a talk with Crystal the other day and told her about you. I see the good things in you that soothe my soul. I don't lose my temper as much with you in my life. I felt guilt that I wasn't home to protect Crystal that night—I guess like Luke felt about Joey, but now I see it wasn't Luke's fault any more than mine for Crystal's death. There are just bad things that happen in life that we can't control." They reach the car, and he opens the door for her.

"You're right, Richard," she says as she seats herself, "like Jesús with his eyesight. But a good thing happened to him." She waits until Richard sits behind the steering wheel. "Richard about you and me. I want one more sign, since you and Crystal were so close, I need one more sign that she would be okay about us. I got one already from the God that holds the universe—not what's in my locket. He did it at the dock. I know He will show us another sign, and it will prove He is real."

"Okay, Jerri, it won't be easy, but I will wait for that. We are almost to your house now. I'll bet Jan will be so happy to see you she may pee herself," Richard laughs.

"Don't laugh, Richard, because she has peed herself before. She's a very happy girl." Jerri laughs, too, "I miss her as well. She's my sunshine."

"She has been a busy girl lately," Richard offers, "with the stables and the charity. It is moving along fast. She and Luke are a good fit together. Their strengths and weaknesses are the opposite, so they lift each other up in a perfect balance. And they are so much fun to watch—the way they tease each other in a playful way. They will never hurt the other's feelings. I think they are falling in love, Jerri, and they have started to attend Ocean Crest Community Church on Sundays."

"Did they say why?"

"Yes. Luke wanted to go, because he can't read his

mom's Book, but he said they will tell him what it says."

Jerri nods, "Oh, now I understand."

Richard continues, "The Ocean Crest Polo Club has planned a ribbon cutting ceremony in two weeks for the Crystal, Joey and Sara Foundation for Disabled Children at the stables, I've been asked to speak. Luke will also be honored, and his story will be told. They'd better hand out tissues for that!"

* * * * *

The time arrives to spread Crystal's ashes in the sea. Richard and Jerri pull into the stables and saddle the horses. Bentley fixes his eyes on the saddle bags. He nuzzles them with his nose and looks at Richard. "Yes, Bentley, that's your momma in there." A tear wells up in Richard's eye, and Bentley whinnies softly.

"Bentley, she's going to ride you to the surf this one last time." Bentley seems to understand.

Jerri mounts Bentley, and Richard throws the saddle bags over Bentley's back before he mounts Tux. They walk slowly down the path to the ocean at sunset. They wade their horses into the surf right at the time the sun is setting on the ocean—just waiting to fall in. The ocean stays calm as they wade out, and Richard reaches for the saddle bags lifting them off Bentley. He removes the plastic bag of ashes. He holds it in his hands. "Jerri, Crystal's journey is almost complete,"

As Richard slowly pours out her ashes, mixed with his tears, gently into the sea, he whispers, "It's over, Sweetheart, for you and me. You now, finally, are free in your sea."

Her ashes turn the ocean into a bright turquoise color.

The horses nod their heads yes and snort.

Jerri puts her Agape glasses on to see. "Richard, is this Crystal standing on the water?"

"What are you seeing?"

"Richard, put your glasses on!"

"Yes! It's her! Crystal!" he shouts.

Crystal's image appears right in front of them, but no voice is heard, she smiles at Jerri and signs to her, "Love him; love each other." Then she blows Richard a kiss and signs to him one last time, "I love Jesus, and I love you. I am with Jesus now," as her image slowly fades away.

"Jerri, this is our sign that we are to be together!" Richard shouts. "Crystal is right about Jesus. Do you want to spend our lives together—just Him and you and me?"

Jerri smiles and says, "At sea I saw the night heavens spread to infinity so I know the God of signs can't be contained in this little locket." She tosses it into the sea.

She pulls Bentley close to Tux saying, "I am not so much a church goer. I have done things I am ashamed of, made so many mistakes in my past. I am skeptical that Crystal's Jesus would ever want to forgive me, but if Jesus is the love in that locket heart, I want that love in mine. Maybe someone, someday, will show me the way to this saved life, like you said Richard before about this born again thing. But as for us, Richard, I know together we are meant to be."

They lean in across their horses for a kiss as the sun gently sinks into the sea.

#

<u>Life Choices</u>

115

I will stop writing here and leave some pages blank.
This story's not over. There are life choices to make.
Inferno everlasting or paradise though the small gate.
If I write the future now, it may be a mistake.
Two life paths before us; what one will you take?

116

117